De-Evolution

FEMINISM'S REVERSE ENGINEERING OF AMERICAN WOMEN

D1717786

COACH GREG ADAMS

ISBN: 978-1-7330396-9-7
ISBN-13:

DEDICATION

This is dedicated to the one and only #coachgang.
Thank you for all of your support and motivation
to keep this message going. Peace!

CONTENTS

FEMINISM (n). The pursuit of equal rights for women at the expense of men

For the definition of terms that I mention in this book please visit: www.gregadamsone.com/dictionary

INTRODUCTION

What started as a need for rights for women has slowly evolved into the longest Civil War in American history. The civil war between men and women is not a physical war. It has been a slow, monotonous, step-by-step psychological war designed to make legislative changes that strip away the rights, wealth and status of men and transfer it to women. This war has been said to be about equality in opportunities but has transformed into emotionally charged debates about equality of outcome, desiring to cherry-pick the highlight reel of a small percentage of men, without accepting the risk, accountability and responsibility necessary to maintain the outcomes.

The original fight was for women's civil and voting rights but it has evolved into more of a women's empowerment movement, emboldening women to possess and display their sexuality and dictate sweeping evolutionary changes that are only advantageous to women.

This movement has led women into the workplace starting around the 1940s, where a group of women would substitute for men in factories producing bombs, tanks, ships, and airplanes while a larger group of men were fighting and dying during World War II. The discovery that women could do a portion of the work that men were doing, as well as earning wages high enough to make them independent, sowed the seeds for the women's movement that we have today. However, the short-sighted misstep of this discovery was that while women could do these jobs in a temporary, need-based capacity, men were REQUIRED to do these job for years and decades and the true demands of the jobs were never tested on women before they began pushing for more roles in the workplace. The poster child for this period was a character known as Rosie The Riveter and she is symbolic for displaying the strength that women needed to do "men's work" in wartime. It depicts a Caucasian woman wearing a red polka dot bandana and a blue work shirt, rolling up her sleeve and displaying her flexed muscle with a defiant and proud scowl, with the inspirational tagline underneath crying "We Can Do It!" This image painted by J. Howard Miller was never intended for public display, however, it became a feminist symbol for many women. While the inspiration for the character has been disputed by a couple of women, it is believed that the actress who portrayed Rosie, actually quit her job after two weeks because of the physical demands.

When men returned from the war, they also returned to discover that many of the factory jobs had machines completing them with greater efficiency and the demand for hard labor decreased while the demand for engineering and building increased. Many women also returned back to the home, assuming the position of primary homemaker and this would lead to a massive increase in the birth rate, the baby boom, in our country.

By the 1950s, families began to escape the heavilly populated cities and headed to the safe and clean suburbs of America. Thus, the American housewife was born. At the time, families were able to thrive off of one income and that income usually was provided by the man and women stayed home or worked part-time to focus on raising the young children. Families across racial and economic lines followed this traditional model of the family support system, with Black American families leading all racial groups of having the most married homes.

Companies would create and market their products based on this model and many of the images that are rejected as oppressive reminders of the women of yesterday were creations of Madison Avenue marketing campaigns.

But, a counter-culture was brewing in these traditional homes as many of the younger girls of the household, the daughters of the housewives would begin to resent their mothers and would vow to never be like them. What they wanted was freedom and liberation. What they got was a sexual revolution.

By the time the 1960s rolled around, the sexual revolution, free love, drugs, and rock-and-roll were in full swing. The younger girls and boys began to participate in what were seen as rebellious activities and it led to major changes in thought and ideology regarding expression, race, and gender roles. We would see women burn their bras to symbolize their freedom from the oppressive Patriarchy and men's sexual expectations of them. Issues regarding abortion, birth control and women in the workplace began to heat up. More women would attend colleges and universities to prepare themselves for careers and young boys were caught in between toiling in blue-collar professions, attending college, engaging in misfit culture or coming in and out of several wars, fighting when they didn't desire to fight.

Feminism would begin to put important legislation into the legal system that would impact America for decades. In June 1963, President John F. Kennedy would sign the Equal Pay Act that was aimed at abolishing wage disparity based on sex. A debate would rage on for another 60 years on whether women receive equal pay, despite it actually being illegal long ago.

The job industry was also changing from factories and

plants to the nice air-conditioned rooms of corporate office buildings. In order to compete in the labor force, women no longer needed to use wrenches or rivets, they could sit behind the typewriter and organize their bosses' schedule, fulfilling a role that these business owners and managers needed, all while sitting in the comfort and protection of a sanitized environment. Many office romances would spark from these working relationships and men with status often became targets of younger women who sought to elevate their status through these relationships. Many men, whether married or single, could easily sell these young women a dream of promised opportunities or perhaps a comfortable life in the suburbs. However, if the dream didn't pan out, it was often the woman that lost out, whether in the form of her employment, reputation, or status. These young women would begin to see men claim jobs and positions that were higher in rank than theirs, or positions they were promised by the bosses that they chose to sleep with. Women saw a chance to get more, not on the battlefield fighting and sacrificing, but in comfortable corporate facilities that would later become the battleground for positions and resources.

During the same decade, the Civil Rights Movement was wrapping up and the leaders were beginning to be killed off. Lyndon Baines Johnson, who was the president that followed John F. Kennedy, would do a number on the black community and every poor community in the United States. He is alleged to have said, "I'll have these Ni**ers voting Democrats for the next 200 years." Essentially, what Lyndon Baines Johnson did with the Civil Rights Act, with the agreement of Martin Luther King, and other civil rights leaders was that he went door-to-door, handing out benefits to the community. Benefits that many in the community today still expect from the United States government. This door-to-door sales campaign would incentivize women to have more children and fewer men in their homes in exchange for resources, government programs, and job placement. Black people at this point in history went from the most married people in the country, at a 70% marital rate to 40 years later, 70% single mother-led households! Maybe Lyndon Johnson was right. He would have these "Negros" voting Democrat, at least for the next 50+ years, with his historic Civil Rights Act.

As women started to advance further in their careers, by the 1970s they started focusing more on their jobs and less on their home. Shows like Mary Tyler Moore and Julia, featuring Diane Carroll, would begin to show images of women "succeeding" in working and child-raising capacities, without men in their homes. The message was clear: be willing to accept the demands from bosses but resent the demands from their husbands. Women would by so doing, inadvertently accept their new Master.

Around the same time, "No-Fault divorce" was initiated in many states in our country. These states begin to accept no-fault divorce as the way for women to leave their husbands legally, without providing proof or an excuse. It didn't matter whether or not the woman was to blame. She could be the abusive one for all intents and purposes, but none of that mattered. "No-fault divorce" changed everything as it allowed women to collect child support and alimony from the husband by initiating it. Today, women file eight out of every ten divorce cases in the United States and in the 40 years since no-fault divorce became the accepted way to end marriages, women receive full custody at an 83% rate and 93% of the child support recipients are women. No-fault divorce changed everything!

The "I Don't Need No Man" culture was born. It would thrive in the culture via music and movies and it became an anthem for many women, especially in the black community. Not surprisingly, white women would catch up some 15 years later, as the television projected Oprah Winfrey and other daytime talk shows into the traditional households of America, filling their heads up with the visions of being controlled by their husbands and chained to their beds. Divorce would rise from 10% to 50% within a 50 year period.

Even more legislation was enacted in favor of women's equity, specifically the Equal Rights Amendment in 1972 (proposed, but never ratified), Title IX (of the education amendments) in 1972, The Equal Employment Opportunities Act in 1972 which lay the groundwork for affirmative action and Roe v. Wade in 1973 which protected women's ability to have an abortion without government restrictions.

Claims of sexual harassment in the workplace also rose and from the 1980s, these claims would cost business owners and managers everything, even though most times, these claims could not be verified.

We began to celebrate the single mother as a hero in the community and at the same time, we began to belittle the so-called "deadbeat dad," who was driven from the home following the Civil Rights Acts and institutionalized welfare programs. Some men were made to pay up to 50% of their income and property to the mother, who traded a father's presence for resources to use at her discretion and used family courtrooms to limit fathers' access to their children for higher child support payment.

By the 1990s, men would go back to war in the desert,

while other men, specifically black men started going to college at record rates. They took less skilled white-collar professions in the hope that they can sit in the boardroom, seeking advancement and promotion. They saddled themselves with debt and began competing with women in the office. This competitive element would spill into romantic relationships, creating palpable tension that today can be described as a wedge between the sexes. Affirmative action programs were in full swing to "correct" the past wrongs and discriminatory hiring practices of yesteryear. Female and male minorities would jockey for positions that white males were being squeezed out of. Minority women that could fill two quotas would benefit the most from this environment, with white women pulling up a close second as Human Resources departments were being ushered into corporations around the country, essentially policing their hiring practices. Minority men, who couldn't fill multiple quotas began to lose out on opportunities compared to their female counterparts, while white men who weren't squeezed out earlier, became targets of claims that made it easier for them to be disposed of.

Meanwhile, at-home, MTV and the public school began to raise our kids. The children of the 1990s would go home to be latchkey kids, while dad and mom jockeyed for jobs and careers. Grunge and hip-hop music would raise this generation with styles that were emotional and hypersexual. Many children had no men in the home, so boys could no longer model what it was like to be a man or what it was like to be a husband. They only had fictional televisions shows like Leave It To Beaver re-runs or the Cosby Show to get a glimpse of what a traditional home looked like. What about the girls? The girls became all too comfortable with having no father around to provide protection, direction, and care. As a result, teenage pregnancy and abortions would skyrocket and the rate of unwed mothers would go from 5% in the 1960s to 45% nationwide.

The adults on the dating market today consist of women who are saddled with college debt, overworked and underpaid, single mothers and/or women who divorce-raped their previous husbands. Thanks to sexual liberation and online dating apps, these leftover women have flooded the market with P-sleeve, driving down the need for men to be involved in committed long-term relationships. What awaits these women are men who have been divorce-raped, disenfranchised by the family court system, saddled with debt, forced to compete with women in the workplace, men who have had restricted access to their children and forced to pay child support at unreasonable rates. There's also the men that they dream of and the rest of the men that they would never even consider, the so-called losers or economically unattractive men. These dating apps are now filled with profiles of thousands of women who essentially have a list of demands, filled with a lot of what they want to receive, but it is not really clear on what they are willing to provide. However, when men provide a list of standards and expectations that they want women to live up to, it is often met with disdain and charges of being misogynistic become the order of the day. In other words, women are able to make demands of men, but men shouldn't dare make demands of women.

The normal living condition for women today is either living with roommates, with a boyfriend, with siblings, their adult children, their parent(s), with pets, or living in properties that men once owned. It is rare to see a traditional married couple living together, except those that have chosen to follow the traditional family model that was popularized in the 1950's media.

Men have been disenfranchised by the Civil Rights Act, the child support services, the family court, and child protective services. Many men have attempted marriage in order to hearken back the times of old and to create stable families, but no-fault divorce, women competing in the workplace, women's right to vote, the dependency on government programs, sexual liberation, legit and false sexual harassment claims, economic disasters, false sense of entitlement and advances in technology with online and mobile dating apps have driven a wedge between men and women. Women want to compete against men, while men don't see a need to compete against women. Neither needs each other and neither can support each other. Women want men for what they can provide and men don't see a need for women for longer than 15 minutes. Women don't need men and men have started to go their own way. Marriage is now obsolete outside of the family raising needs and unnecessary for both.

With this amount of so-called progress, we have lost more than we could ever potentially gain. My question is... Was it worth it?

PART

I

FEMINISM IS CANCER

CHAPTER

1

WOMEN BASHING

WARNING: If you're a snowflake or a man or woman that will get their feelings hurt easily in the face of truth, data and verified evidence, just leave right now. Don't come back to me later to tell me that you don't like the way I made you feel about some of the things that we can plainly see today. If you want to hear a side of an argument that is being censored and de-platformed because it doesn't follow the segment of society that wishes it were different, then stick around. Otherwise, leave now! You were warned.

I can write entire books about some of the deplorable things that men have done to society. The fact is, many people have already written about them, but what people refuse to let happen is a book written completely about women and the despicable behaviors that we have allowed to take root and flourish. As soon as you're not raining praise, accolades and empowering phrases upon women, they want you to be silent. They redirect the conversation back to men "well, men do it too," or "that goes both ways," similar to what a 2nd grader would say when someone is holding them accountable for behaviors that they should change. I've noticed that when women are receiving positive attention, they never invite men into the conversation, but when they have to be held accountable for their actions, all of a sudden they want men to share the limelight.

Worse still, the white knighting men who will step forward to defend the honor of women that they don't even know, ready to pepper me with all of the predictable emotional terms that they think women would say, so they can collect the accolades of strangers, like a proud puppy pleasing its owner.

I am looking to bring an intelligent and rational conversation to the table about a system that is obviously broken. Any movement that claims to fight for equality for women but doesn't at least offer to give up the advantages that they have over men (i.e., in the family court or being required to register for Selective Services) is fraudulent by definition. You cannot have a divorce rate approaching 60% and single motherhood rate approaching 50% nationally and continue to look at men as the problem. I don't berate or call women names and those that speak to me without allowing their emotions to well up often find that we agree on more points than we disagree. When I am dismissed as a misogynist because of my beliefs and women shut down the conversation, the conversation doesn't end. It continues well beyond that, only with men who are really misogynists. If only the men who hate women and the rational, intelligent men are having the conversation, the gap will never be bridged.

For the sake of understanding, I'm going to present my best "my friend is black, so I can't be racist" argument that I can, to attempt to alleviate your belief that I'm a woman basher.

Women have been very instrumental in all aspects of my life, my family, my career, and my businesses. Believe it or not, there are women that have championed my efforts to spread this message. They understand that they may not agree with all of my positions, but that the passion to pursue truth was more important than their feelings.

I've also had what could be best described as exceptional short- term, non-monogamous relationships with women. Especially with those who accepted the philosophy that I outlined in my first book *Free Agent Lifestyle*, which are the three tenants of male freedom; No cohabitation, no long term relationships, and no marriage.

During my career as a women's college basketball coach, four different women have hired me as an assistant coach, three of them being African-American. While I was working as a fitness trainer in southern California, 65-70% of my clientele were women who used their families' discretionary income to support the service that I was providing. They were very dedicated and loyal to me and extended gifts to my family which proved to be beyond beneficial, as I was trying to grow my business and while my family was going through an awful divorce. One client was instrumental in providing admission opportunities to a prestigious private high school for my children.

Oh, and I shouldn't forget to tell you, that my mother is a woman and so are my four aunts, my four sisters and many of my matriarchal cousins. A vast majority of them support my ability to extend this message without feeling the need to support my every word.

It is important to note that when I talk about women, I am discussing their nature. Many of these qualities are in them whether they are related to me, support me or outrightly ignore me. It isn't meant to paint those that I know negatively, it is only meant to describe them. Some women may fall into the "exception to the rule" category.

Some of them have suppressed their nature well enough so it doesn't interfere with our working or business arrangement. The same can be said for me. In order to make my relationships work, both must be willing to cooperate or meet in the middle to make the relationship beneficial.

This is where most women get it wrong. Today's women do not want to meet in the middle. They seek neither fairness nor equality. They seek dominance and they wish for men to hand all of it to them. They only want equal rights when it benefits them. In other words, they're strident feminists until it's time to pay the bill.

If you can't criticize and question an idea without being ostracized, you know something isn't right.

SHUTTING UP IS WHAT GOT US HERE

When men have issues in their lives, they want us to talk about them to try to find solutions. When the issue is a woman in their life, it's a non-versation, because men's issues should not include women as the problem. The truth is, men are having problems with women and most of their issues stem from their interactions and relationships with them.

One of the criticisms that I received in the past two years of creating content for men is "Why do I continue to talk about women when we have gone our own way or are focusing on doing our own thing?

The first thing to understand about this type of criticism is that it is more of a demand than it is a question. Usually, when someone asks a question, they usually intend to receive information that would allow for a better understanding. In today's sensitive and censorship climate where one side wants to control the narrative, questions are not asked for better understanding, they are formed to criticize and make demands.

So the original question posed is not "Why do you continue to talk about women..." Rather it is a demand to stop talking about women because what I'm saying is true and that truth should be silenced.

This is very important to understand. Much of my content is talking about the conditioning that is being dispensed in media, music, and entertainment that places women high upon a pedestal. We're told to approach them, start conversations, ask for dates and if we don't, we're quitters who don't have any game, while at the same time risking being accused of sexual harassment or being a thirsty beta male if we do approach. These mixed messages are used to shame men back into approaching, putting the ball back into women's court, placing all of the risk, accountability, and responsibility on men.

Men are told that showering them with attention, gifts, cash, and prizes is a one-way ticket to happiness for all involved. Once you do those things and they don't work out, whether in a short-term or long-term relationship, she's able to leave men holding the bag of that failed relationship.

These are the things that dating coaches and pick-up artists don't address. They simply use the same emotional tactics that society uses to get you back on the field using these archaic mating rituals. Men take the blame for failed relationships and become the punching bag of their family, friends, and society.

As the dynamics of relationships between men and

women are changing, men are seeking solutions to these issues, to provide clarity and understanding of why these things continue to happen. The solutions that are offered to men are "find another one" and "try a little bit harder next time." Try a little bit harder than you did the last time even though you might have very well given your best effort.

Society is very different today because men are now discussing their relationships in public forums and on platforms like YouTube and Instagram. What once was considered off-limits or demoralizing to discuss, is now fair game and men are seeing a lot more commonalities in regard to destructive female behavior and they are rallying around each other. Unfortunately, society is slow to recognize this and is providing old solutions to new problems, like an uncle performing magic tricks to his teenage nieces and nephews. What used to leave them in awe is falling flatter than a pancake. The solution to "dust yourself off and try again" is just not going to fly when hundreds of thousands of men are discovering that they aren't the only ones.

Even though I have decided to close the possibility of cohabitation, marriage, and long-term relationships, I think it's beneficial for us to continue to talk about women because it humanizes them, it removes the mystique, it corrects the sugar-and-spice conditioning that many of us learned that has allowed women to manipulate men in relationships. I use my platform to present statistical data and factual evidence to de-pedestalize women for the men who are one blow job away from returning to the plantation. With the media continuing to place this shroud of mystery and an era of mystique around women, there is a need for men like me to show through statistics, that you might be better off paying more attention to your own life than investing too much of your energy and effort into women.

This is the Free Agent Lifestyle! Once men start living for themselves and not the validation from women, what they will discover is what the men before us already knew. They already removed the mystique from women based on the number of women that they were exposed to. They knew well before us that the vast majority of women weren't worth the investment of emotions, finances, time, commitment and sacrifice that many suggest is needed to win them over. These men got the absolute best out of them at the best time of their lives, without giving up anything. They considered women's emotions secondary and quite honestly all people should take this approach. The minute you prioritize the opinions of others before yours, you'll find yourself living the life that they want instead of the life that you want for yourself.

We have a lot of issues in our society that we wish would change and go away, like homelessness, drug abuse, and bullying, but we don't ignore them because they are real issues in our lives. So, we continue to talk about them until enough people are willing to provide real solutions because we know that ignoring it won't change them or make them go away.

Women are free to discuss issues that affect them, which ultimately brings male behavior into the discussion. Whether it's rape, sexual assault, the #metoo movement or workplace harassment, they are constantly talking about these issues because they want to change it or see them go away. Talking about it creates an impact and seeks to cause a change in the people who are contributing to the behavior. These issues that women are discussing almost always involve men. However, we don't openly shame women for talking about an issue that they want to see change. We don't call them names, claim that they're hurt just to dismiss the issue or turn their issues into issues that men have. We are expected to deal with them and find solutions. Unfortunately, men are not afforded the same when they are the victims.

The message is clear: Women seek praise only. They don't want criticism or to be corrected when they're wrong. They don't want to be told that they are the cause of an issue or that their behavior must change. They want to dictate what needs to be changed around them and WHO should change it for them. When they turn on their TVs and movies, they find people praising them. They turn on their radios and people are praising them. They load up their dating apps and social media accounts and there are people praising them. They are in a constant state of receiving praise for doing the simplest of tasks.

However, when they receive criticism based on facts that can be shown, they want you to be silent. "Be quiet, we don't want to hear any criticism about ourselves, in fact, what we're going to do is silence you. What we're going to do is complain about you. We're going to de-platform and censor you from social media sites to prevent you from spreading your criticism. We're going to ridicule and call you names in order to keep you quiet."

The message for men is that women need you to be available to be easily manipulated at their discretion. And, if you don't cooperate or be willing to be manipulated, they need you to just shut up and disappear.

Fortunately, there are more men willing to talk. We are literally breaking the social conditioning that has allowed predatory women to thrive. We break the programming, so it is important that we discuss women, even in the face of being called a WOMAN BASHER. The reality is that shutting up is what got us in this position in the first place. Our fathers, our grandfathers, and our Uncle Simps were the men who shut up when it didn't go well for them in Family Court. They were the ones who shut up when it didn't go well for them in the child support court. They were the ones who shut up when they were getting the short end of the stick in relationships and marriage. And look at where we are today!

Those men shut up and affected the rest of the men that are in this problem today. At the end of the day, we have the right to talk about whomever or whatever it is that we want to talk about. We're here sharing for other men. We're not here to discuss this issue for men who aren't willing to receive this message. We're not here to discuss these issues for women who want men to be the deaf, dumb and blind lemming that will comply with their every whim.

Men are able to have standards and expectations of women since we are the gatekeepers to relationships. It is not WOMAN BASHING if women are choosing not to put their best foot forward and meet those expectations. For men who are able to control their thirst and libido, they will find that being more selective and patient will yield them much better results and the number of toxic women that are on the prowl for beta simps will be filtered from them.

If people believe that men placing standards and expectations on women is WOMAN BASHING, then the rest of this book will be a complete therapy bashing session. Many of these issues that I discuss are not the result of things that pop up in my head. I have taken time

23

to research the issue and present the evidence before I openly discuss it. Unfortunately, this just comes off as WOMEN BASHING.

CHAPTER

2

ELEVEN PREDICTABLE REBUTTALS

I have been speaking out on these issues and making social commentary videos on social media for the past five years and believe me, I've heard just about every emotion-based objection that can possibly be raising. Most, if not all, range between fear-based declarations to emotional, shame-based comments. The only thing that would surprise me is if someone actually disagreed with every notion that I present and disputed them with a rational idea of their own.

When men seek to come to the table with their ideas on how to improve the ideology of feminism, they are easily dismissed and labeled. And even though to some, my approach may seem harsh, I have always said that I would be willing to meet in the middle regarding solution-based legislation and real equitable treatment between the sexes. The problem is that feminists are dismissive of men like me who are actually willing to bend so society doesn't break. We are only able to share these ideas behind closed doors with other men who are a lot less forgiving. This doesn't close the rift, it widens it.

I can say this for sure, those who disagree with my stance are going to use every way to discredit me by bringing emotional-based arguments into the discussion, or name-calling or pure judgment. Feelings override facts unfortunately and every step will be taken by the "feelings police" to not confront the evidence that I present. I have given full-hour presentations in front of large groups in order to find some common ground in relationships or to shed light on issues, only to find the questions and answer segment filled with nothing more than an elementary school playground argument. These questions never dispute the evidence, nor do they move us any closer to resolving the issue. It actually drives us farther apart by projecting their emotional statements to very important issues.

So, I've already taken the guesswork out for these people and offered these eleven predictable objections and tactics that are used against me. I've heard all of these and guess what, it hasn't changed my opinion one bit. It actually bolsters my argument and lets me know that I have been knocking at the right door.

These programmed responses are what they've heard in movies and in the media and they all sound the same, word for word, with the same inflection and tempo. Even in written form, the response always looks the same. For instance, "Who Hurt You" will always be followed by a laughing emoji or LMAO/Lol. There will be no disputing the argument, no suggestion that they really want to know who the person is that allegedly hurt me, nor will there be an actual concern for my emotions. It's an attack, but not a thoughtful attack. It's a programmed response that doesn't address the issue, it changes the subject from the issue back to me or is intended to make me feel like the issue only affects me. Interestingly, the number of people who follow me would suggest otherwise.

Without further ado, here are the eleven most predictable objections that I will hear from detractors.

1. "You HATE women!"/"What Kind Of Women Are You Meeting?"/"Where Are You Meeting These Women?"

This is a very disingenuous argument and quite frankly it insults my intelligence. It suggests that an adult woman has been able to successfully go through life without ever encountering any deceitful women. Just going through middle school alone would expose you to fifty! And another hundred in high school, and another thousand in college. They've managed to make movies, music, books, religion, the freakin' Holy bible, failed friendships, reality shows, and every popular social media app. One could find examples of women behaving badly in all of these. This individual is claiming to be completely oblivious to any of this! Watch movies like Mean Girls, The Crush, Single White Female, Thin Line Between Love & Hate, Basic Instinct, Fatal Attraction or Hand That Rocks The Cradle and you will see women depicted as vindictive, narcissistic, abusive, and controlling. Somehow, they've been living in a cave and I'm apparently making it all up. Either way, it is a gaslighting tactic meant to change the subject matter to me rather than the evidence in an effort to make me question my own sanity.

2. Exception To The Rule

Unfortunately, I can only speak very broadly about this subject and I don't have enough pages to talk about every single person in America. Since that's the case, someone will inevitably bring up one or two examples of people that they know that the rule doesn't apply to in an attempt to discredit the rule. The reality is, there is no rule, there are some people and there are most people. Sure, there are going to be some outliers that do not fit the picture that I have painted, but most people fit it perfectly. For instance, in regards to single-mother households, children raised in single mother-led homes are more susceptible to a variety of social pitfalls compared to children raised in dual-parent households. The statement alone is accurate, it is supported by verifiable evidence and more single mother-led households experience these issues than don't. However, instead of agreeing with the evidence and accepting that children are more at risk, someone will bring up the story of one middle-class single mother-led household that they know whose son went to Yale law school and became the President of the United States. That household would fit in with the statistical outlier and wouldn't be the case 99.9% of the time. It would be dangerous for us to believe that every single mother-led household could achieve outlier status. Maybe there was a lot of luck involved or someone was there to provide an opportunity for the son that wasn't available for everyone else, but the exception does not disprove the evidence.

3. "Who Hurt You?"

I touched on this earlier but this one has deflection, projection, and gaslighting written all over it, and it's passive-aggressive, to say the least. We often disguise clear and direct accusations behind questions that clearly cannot be answered because they aren't actually questions that someone wants answers to. The question means to say "It is clear that somebody hurt you." But they can't say that because they have no evidence to prove their statement. When posed as a question, the questioner doesn't intend to stick around to hear an answer to the question. They really don't want to know precisely "Who Hurt You" but they are willing to project their emotional approach to dealing with tough situations onto you. 90% of those who use this objection will be women and 10% will be men who were more likely raised by women. Questions like these never move the conversation forward. They actually pull the conversation back and it's a solid, yet weak tactic to use when you don't intend to meet a person's expectations.

4. "You're just bitter"

This statement is better than the previous objection simply because it is direct. But, the issue with it is that it is accusatory and cannot be proven. Based on the fact that 99% of relationships fail and 67% of marriages fail, to assume that someone is bitter because of failed relationships is a half-truth at best. At worst, it's a projection, a statement that concludes how the accuser handles situations, but not how I handle situations. To handle this objection, I would have to change the subject matter back to me and my personal relationships to ferret out where the bitterness came from instead of dealing with the original point. Like most of the other statements, this actually affirms my position because this one specifically is an admission that women can be predatory and manipulative. So when men speak out against it, they are emotional about it and no one cares about men's emotions unless they can benefit from them.

5. "You Can't Get Women/Women Don't Want You/ That's Why You're Still Single"

I'm surprised women can say this to me with a straight face, but that hasn't stopped a few from trying. With the open sexual marketplace and the number of women jumping on and off the cock carousel, it would be impossible for me to not stumble across a woman with even the most minimal effort. So this one is a way to switch the subject back to me, rather than the original subject. To highlight subjective qualities that they don't find attractive but others do, doesn't prove that I'm incorrect. In fact, all I would need to do is produce one woman in 4 billion to disprove their claim. But, would my time be better suited proving them wrong or proving my original statements right? If I spend time trying to prove that I can actually get women, they have successfully diverted the conversation from something that they didn't want to discuss to something completely irrelevant. Additionally, women are the gatekeepers to sex and men are the gatekeepers of all relationships. When a man is single it is by choice. Women decide when they open their legs. Men decide when they open their wallets.

6. NAWALT - Not All Women Are Like That

When debating women, this is about as close to admission to my statements as we will possibly get about women's unperfection. It also combines the Exception To The Rule argument, as well. This is the equivalent of saying "You are correct and, although 90% of women are like that, please consider the 10% of women that aren't." And, I would admit that they may be correct, except for this important fact. When men are discussing predatory women capitalizing on the archaic family court laws, we are essentially saying that not all women WOULD do this, but all women COULD do this. So, it is much safer to assume that they will rather than they won't.

7. "You're just not meeting the right women"

The ole, "keep trying until you find the right woman." Very similar to the "where are you finding these women" question, mixed with a little "not all women are like that." Listen, if there is a commonly held secret as to where all of these good women are, let them be revealed today or forever hold your peace. Unfortunately, women are like Blow Pops. You have to do a lot of licking to get to the gum in the middle and even that's a sticky situation. It's also not really a solution to the issue of the unfairness in family court laws and feminist ideology either. Finding the "right woman" still leaves men exposed to the dangers of an abusive marriage, sexless marriage, divorce, and the family court. In fact, 2nd and 3rd marriages are statistically worse than the 1st.

8. Attack My Masculinity (Gay/Incel)

Welcome to 5th grade, everyone! Where we can challenge your sexuality and masculinity so you can change your opinion about women. In today's climate, society is way more sympathetic to gay men than they are straight men. So, it would be a benefit for a person to come out as gay, rather than putting up with ad hominem attacks from just about everyone. Women have traditionally aligned with gay men and gay men have benefited from feminist ideology. It makes no sense for a gay man to be hiding under anti-feminist thought. If they really thought the person was gay, this would actually be considered a hate crime. Many men that share in this philosophy often come from heterosexual relationships that ended in divorce, custody battles and child support issues, so there goes the Incel argument. Nonetheless, it is an attempt to change the subject matter, sidetrack the discussion and provoke emotions.

9. GASLIGHTING. "You're crazy"

This is perhaps the most dangerous of the objections because it challenges a person's mental stability and many men in relationships allow the people that they care about the most to use this tactic at the expense of their mental health. Only to find out over time, that their suspicions were valid. This is a complete mindf*ck. However, in regard to my content, gaslighting is an avoidance tactic to make it seem like I am living in a parallel universe and that there is no way that these things are true. The problem is, gaslighting never disproves my point. It only misdirects the discussion and drives away the possibility of bridging any gaps. For them, it's better for them to make us think that we're crazy, rather than addressing the issues rationally.

10. Red herring/straw man fallacy

The red herring is basically trying to misdirect the argument into another. An example of this is when a woman is asked a question that she may be guilty of and she answers with "How could you ask me that question?" Or, if you spy on a spouse's phone and find that they are cheating, they may say "I can't believe that you would spy on me." Nevermind the fact that they got caught red-handed, now you are trying to defend why it was an ethical way to catch someone violating the terms of your agreement. The straw man is the attacking of one weakness in your argument and turning the entire discussion on that one point while avoiding the stronger, more relevant points. For instance, if I say that the majority of women are overweight because of a lack of exercise and addiction to chocolate chip cookies, the obvious point of contention would be whether women are addicted to chocolate chip cookies. They will ask for charts, graphs and data regarding chocolate chip cookie consumption and completely ignore the fact that there is data that proves that the majority of women are in fact overweight. The profile of the average American woman is 5'4" and 168lbs. Lack of prolonged exercise is very easy to prove as well, however, no attention will be paid to those facts and now, the entire point and discussion has been nullified simply because you got caught up in a discussion regarding chocolate chip cookies.

11. "That Goes Both Ways"

Remember when I discussed women and praise? This is that moment. When there is praise for women, they rarely open the door to invite men in praise receiving. But, when there is criticism, let's turn all of that attention back to men. In other words, since "Men do it too" the behavior that they are being called out on should be excused. While it may be true that "men do it too," we are talking about women right now. Please stay on the subject.

The reality is, relationships have become a one-sided deal because women feel entitled to receive all of the benefits associated with the union and provide very little in return. The old narrative that men should just be happy or lucky to be in the company of women changed when sexual liberation became the norm. Being in the company of a woman is a very simple task to achieve and men don't consider themselves lucky for just receiving the slightest amount of female attention. Men are starting to vocalize their displeasure with modern women and are starting to set standards for quality women. The time where just any ole women will do does not exist anymore.

When it comes to the expectation for paying for first dates, does that go both ways? What about the stigma of domestic violence? Statistically, women commit domestic violence near the same rate as men, however, it doesn't go both ways in regard to support groups or the expectations for men to deal with it.

What about the fact that women are the recipients of child support in over 80% of the cases and alimony recipients in over 90% of all cases nationwide. That certainly is not going both ways. But, when we bring up these obvious inequities, all of a sudden, I hate women. What about the NON-versation between men and women regarding relationships? Women simply aren't willing to listen to issues that men are having without swinging the conversation back to what they aren't getting, and they have a clear advantage!

This message is loud and clear, men should never expect women to treat them fair in relationships, friendships, and marriage. They want all the advantages without the risk. Since men are the gatekeepers to relationships, men should expect more. Unfortunately, there are simps who will always be willing to accept less.

Now that we've got the simpletons out of the building, let's get down to business.

CHAPTER

3

SCOREBOARD OF FEMINISM

Here are some interesting statistics:
(See the *About The Research* section for source information)

- ❖ 60 million+ abortions since 1973
- ❖ 68% of the U.S student loan debt belongs to women
- ❖ 45% of women age 25-44 work full time
- ❖ 85% of those living paycheck-to-paycheck are women
- ❖ Women are responsible for 73% of consumer spending (U.S)
- ❖ 66% of women carry credit card debt
- ❖ 77% of black children are born to unwed mothers
- ❖ 45% of American children are born to unwed mothers
- ❖ Over half of all U.S marriages will end in divorce
- ❖ 67% of the marriages that ended in divorce lasted 8 yrs or less
- ❖ 80% of divorces are initiated by women
- ❖ 1/4 women take mental health medication
- ❖ 52% of American Women are single

- ❖ The U.S birthrate has declined for four consecutive years
- ❖ 93% of alimony is paid from men to women
- ❖ 83% of women receive primary custody of children
- ❖ 83% of child support payments are paid to women
- ❖ 72% of the inmates in state prison were raised by single mothers

Feminists love stats. Especially those that make their cause look successful. As well as stats that make men look bad. We all know that 50% of husbands cheat, 60% of domestic violence abusers are men and that women make $0.77 on the dollar compared to men. We literally know these stats by heart. But when it comes to stats that reflect poorly on women, all we get is deflection. Not to mention the fact that there are no commercials made about them and no heartfelt news stories that make men the sympathetic heroes for having to overcome these issues. Nope! When feminists see statistics like these, their first thought is to blame men for their own shortcomings. As most of you can see, these stats rarely affect just women. They also affect men, children, and the greater society. I mean, if feminism is really winning, we must be on our way to hell in a handbasket very soon.

I am not going to be nice about it. Feminism took a giant steaming pile of shit on our culture and there have been far more devastating consequences than there have been gains in the last 50 years. I understand that no new revolution goes without its growing pains, however, feminism is a full-grown cancerous tumor and the more it grows, the more men are expected to find solutions to problems that they did not create.

In order for feminism to thrive, it must be supported by colleges and universities, corporations that depend on women trading their fertility for desk jobs, media propaganda, celebrities pushing the agenda, politicians and lobbyist groups, and most importantly, compliant MEN.

No matter how much we hear that women are earning more money, becoming financially independent, and living empowered lives, marriage (or divorce) is STILL the primary way that women become wealthy.

Women have essentially made themselves obsolete with the advance in technology in kitchen appliances, food delivery services and the gig economy where people will do the chores around your house for a fee. Women that chose to re-embrace those roles in time of war, natural disasters and difficult economies will find that their services are no longer needed. When women refused to provide these services at home, men figured it out, did it for themselves and asked: "Is this what they're complaining about?"

When women aren't married, they barely make enough money to care for themselves. They choose jobs and professions that will not make them self-sufficient, rich, or wealthy. They rarely start their own businesses and when they do, they are usually small businesses that employ less than five people. Since they are not getting married to economically attractive men that can care and provide for them well into their older ages, the government has to pick up the tab, and the government will collapse if they have to keep providing programs for women such as Head start for single mothers, welfare, housing vouchers, etc. These are all programs that are predominantly geared towards helping women; the ironically strong and independent women, to maintain just a basic quality of life.

FEMINISM: YOU WERE LIED TO

I know a lot of women will probably not pick up this book and be willing to listen objectively. Those that do may deal with the content with subjective feelings or project their emotions on to me in order to explain my motives. A rare few will be willing to understand because feminism has been as much of a bully to them as it has been to men. But, I've just got to tell you, you've been lied to and it's just unfortunate. You've been sold a fantasy and just like men, you were sold something that really doesn't exist.

If you think about what relationships are or what they were about 200 years ago, relationships were used for the survival of the species. Men and women united to procreate, protect, and provide in order to survive. Families were created in order to produce a legacy. Today, we can create a legacy for ourselves without the need for a family. We can produce a legacy without producing offspring because today, family and relationships are done. They're doomed! They've been destroyed. It's become increasingly difficult for people to have relationships and one of the main reasons for that is that feminism has come in like cancer and destroyed all of the benefits that a male and a female receive from a relationship. The feminist ideology completely fooled women, lying to them about "having it all," receiving a college education and contributing to the family with a "career" all while men conform to the new standards that feminism sets for women.

I am constantly inundated with single females over the age of 35 who believe that they bring something to "the table," enough for me to get emotionally involved with them. Truthfully, these women become the distraction and the obstacle in my life when I try to cultivate legitimate relationships.

Now obviously, they bring that P-sleeve to the table, which may interest me just enough to give them a little quality time, but with my schedule and commitments, that can only interest me so much. I can only take so much time out of my day to chase substandard, non-feminine women. To add to that, with the amount of vagina available on the sexual marketplace, it doesn't take much effort to get it if I need it. It is not just me. I know a lot of men who are dealing with the same situation.

I can already hear all of the women who believe that they have the golden P-sleeve, assuring men that they are worth the wait. Women used to be able to sell this idea when men didn't have so much access to the sex that has flooded the market by single mothers, divorcees, and young thots. But, men have been able to sample so much P-sleeve that we have determined that there is not much difference between one and the other. Sure, there may be more of an attraction to the face that is attached to the P-sleeve but not that big of a difference that he would wait longer than three weeks to get it. If she is making him wait for it, it probably isn't worth it.

As men and women get older, the roles in the sexual marketplace reverse. At a young age, women are getting inundated by a lot of men who want to be with them, but once they hit the age of 35, the advantage on the marketplace begins to favor the men over the age of 35. Then, the men are getting inundated with women offering themselves to men, in exchange for...not much.

Delusional women who've lost their advantage in the marketplace believe that qualities that feminism has emphasized will bring men running to them. But, they find out the hard way that it's a lie, and go on for the next 15 years kicking and screaming about their paper degree, series of jobs (career), and financial independence. The lie that feminism told women is that they would be able to obtain equality through a degree and status (male qualities), however, it is not until after they've obtained their degree, locked themselves down with student loan debt and years clocked in cubicles, that they find out that a degree and status mean something for men, but is not always a selling point for women.

Men want women that are supportive and not controlling enough to prevent us from having that which we seek, which is Peace, Quiet, and Freedom. By nature, men are dominant, and successful families have dominant men. A woman who seeks to be dominant in relationships or who wants equal partnerships is a feminist and is to be avoided. There is nothing equal about a partnership and the individual who has the most responsibility or will receive the most blame and criticism for any failures should be dominant. I've often found that the women who attempted to assume the dominant role in their relationship often blame men for shortcomings in the relationship. In times where quick decisions are required, so-called dominant women seem to freeze up or defer, forcing weak men to make critical decisions that he didn't anticipate making, because his "loudmouth" wife had all the answers in comfortable times.

What men must understand is, <u>We Are The Prize</u>, we produce most of the resources and women depend on our provision, safety, and security. It is you that brings validation to their lives because no matter how loud the "I don't need no man" choir sings, women are not validated unless they have a man. If they never get one, they are never validated. For men, there is no woman on this EARTH that can validate them, they can only support his effort and procreate for them. This support is vital; it is necessary and should be rewarded when done properly.

50 YEARS OF FEMINISM, BUT NOTHING IS THEIR FAULT

I realize that no matter how much statistical data and charts that I present in my argument, those that disagree with me will make their argument emotional. They will start their sentence with "Well, as a woman...," then (insert emotional-based argument that disregards any evidence that was presented). That's usually how these things work.

Feminism has been a giant dramatic Sh*t Test against American men. Sadly, American men have bent over and taken it and failed. When we realized that we were going to take the blame for the conditions, even though feminism was at the wheel, we knew we f*cked up. If I'm going to take the blame, at the very least, I should be behind the wheel.

TRENDING UPWARD

All of the evidence that you're going to see has a commonality in the timing of when that trend changed. Since third-wave feminism was installed in the 1960s, we've experienced significant changes in legislation and as a result, every trend that I discuss is going to have an upward trend on the timeline and that trend upward is usually associated with a negative result for society or in relation to men.

In the last one hundred and forty-four years of marriage, the rate of divorce was somewhere around the 9% range in the early nineteen hundreds. Around the 1960s, during the implementation of feminism, there was a large spike in the divorces. Between 1960 and 1972, divorce rates were somewhere around 28%. Today we're well over the reported 50%.

There were also major changes in the labor force during this time. In the 1950s, only around 33% of women aged 16 and older were working outside of the home, with the majority of the work being part-time. By 2017, that number has jumped to 57% and now women make up the majority of the job holders in America. At the same time, men began to lose their position in the labor force. As a result of feminism, more women received jobs but fewer men were working than before. The number of men working went from 86% to below 69%. So, women gained more as a result of feminism but more men lost jobs. At the beginning of this book, I gave you my definition of feminism, which is *the pursuit of equal rights for women, at the expense of men,* and so far these results are holding that to be true. The alternative thinkers will say that there's fewer men motivated to work or less college-educated men but the fact is, when more women entered the workforce, fewer men were able to get jobs.

THE TWO-INCOME TRAP

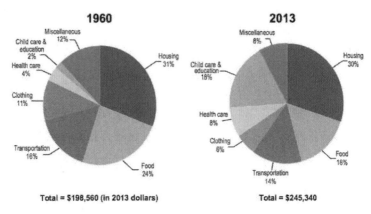

1960

Miscellaneous 12%
Child care & education 2%
Health care 4%
Clothing 11%
Transportation 16%
Housing 31%
Food 24%

Total = $198,560 (in 2013 dollars)

2013

Miscellaneous 8%
Child care & education 18%
Health care 8%
Clothing 6%
Transportation 14%
Housing 30%
Food 16%

Total = $245,340

Expenditures of a child from birth through age 17. Total expenses and budgetary component shares, 1960 versus 2013

To handle the "well, the economy has changed, but wages have been stagnant" excuse-makers, the graphs above discredit that argument. This chart depicts what it cost to raise a kid from birth to 17 in the 1960s and what it costed in 2013. The chart takes inflation into account for those who want to argue that prices in housing and food have changed while wages have stayed the same. If you notice where the biggest difference in cost was experienced from 1960 to 2013, childcare and education had the largest change. Everything else relatively stayed the same. It does cost more to raise children, but not that much and most of that cost can be directly pointed to the increase in child care. But, why did childcare and education go up? Because during that same time, the individual who was providing free childcare left the home to pursue "careers." Feminism loves to champion opportunities and gains for women in the workplace but never calculates the cost of removing both parents from the home. The loss of both parents from the home has been significantly more impactful than women working at a desk. We've paid a significant price for this, a price that will be felt for centuries. That is a direct result of feminism.

Also around the same time, more women began to graduate with college degrees than men. Unfortunately, most of the degrees were obtained in majors that didn't translate into an increased earning potential. What feminism sold to women and minorities to an extent, is that college education is the great equalizer. It would provide a level of status that no one could deny and as a result, the "white male oppressors" would have to promote all degree holders at the same rate. While some people have been able to enter into the workplace with their degree, the vast majority of degree holders don't have jobs where their degree is relevant and they became debt slaves in the process. The truth is, as much as we want to celebrate women graduating college more than men, we have to acknowledge the fact that 67% of the student loan debt in our country today belongs to women and the amount of student loan debt has tripled in the past 18 years. Are we celebrating now?

Sure, women have been able to become more "independent" than they were before and they were able to get more jobs, but the problem that arose was an increase in child care, and the disruption in the family is always understated because nobody's at home raising the children. Both parents are working, but both can barely afford to support the family because of child care and education costs. United States presidential candidate Elizabeth Warren wrote a book called The Two-Income Trap addressing this issue.

THE SINGLE MOTHER PLAGUE

Being a single, unwed mother used to bring shame upon a family. Fathers were well aware that their daughter's marketplace value would plummet if their daughter was known for producing bastard children. This used to be a thing. But, not anymore.

With new "independent" attitudes, sexual liberation, skyrocketing divorce rate and the praising of single mothers as heroes, the number of children born to single mothers grew to levels that were inconceivable a century ago. In the 1950s, just before the installation of feminism, there were close to 5% of children born to single or unwed mothers. Today, well after the installation and permanent residential occupation of feminism, that number has ballooned to over 40%. 40%!!! This is after important legislation such as Roe v. Wade and Affirmative Action laws. This is after massive amounts of abortions, nearly 60 million in the United States and over a billion worldwide.

These are the results of women's empowerment. This is the so-called "it not feminism's fault" results. This is the so-called, "the man ran away from his responsibility." No, 40% of men did not just run away. This is women's inability to handle the sexual liberation responsibly. Women attempting to turn post night club hookups into a traditional family will always backfire and placing the blame on men who were enjoying a night of passion with a sexually liberated woman shows that women have not been able to handle their "liberation" responsibly.

When men were incentivized to be responsible, they did it. They did it when it was actually worth having a family when one man was able to support an entire family without the woman in the household aligning with the feminist ideology to completely undermine his authority.

What has changed is the implementation and the marching in of feminism's ideology, affirmative action, removing fathers from the homes, claiming female supremacy and independence, taking control of their sexuality and reproductive rights and the lack of fathers rights in the family court. The economy hasn't changed as much as these things have. But, of course, feminism ignores these issues or makes an excuse for them altogether.

For the excuse-makers who still say the economy is the issue, it is believed that Americans' paychecks are bigger now than they were 40 years ago, yet people are feeling pinched. As child care increases, so has entitlement. Our consumption of luxury items has become the norm and the average American can somehow afford $1500 cell phones, $200 basketball shoes, and $2000 clutch bags but still can blame the economy for their shortcomings. The average American feels that they deserve a 3200 square foot McMansion as their first home and a luxury car as their first financed vehicle. Women are still able to control 85% of consumer spending in America. So the dollars are there, but greed is what's changed. The entitlement is what changed. The amount of debt that we put on ourselves has changed. The economy has done very well over the last 70 years during the Reign of Feminism, except for a few blips. Women today have more crap than they need, in fact, they have everything, but when it comes to taking the blame for their shortcomings in society, it's not their fault.

If we look at the things that have become more expensive in the last 20 years and look at the things that have become more affordable, you will see who the economy has taken advantage of. Things that typically are bought by men: televisions, toys, computer software, wireless telephone services are more affordable. Even new cars have remained steady based on the amount of dollars available. Of course, luxury vehicles have gone up and since many people want their first car to be a luxury vehicle and not an economy vehicle, they can't believe that vehicle prices have remained steady.

Now, let's take a look at the things that have become more expensive in the last 20 years. College tuition and fees, as a result of people's willingness to pay whatever is needed to go to college, these colleges have raised the price through the roof. The cost of college textbooks has gone up. Hospital services have skyrocketed and the cost of child care services/nursery schools has increased as we discussed earlier. It's easy to see what the economy has adjusted to. This is the supply and demand principle. If there is a demand for more educated women and there are more single/divorced mothers on the market, the economy will be willing to supply the services that they need at premium rates. The markets will take advantage of it. However, it will not be very affordable for one person.

OLDER MOMS

One of my arguments related to feminism is that women are taking their most fertile years, the years that they should be using taking care of and raising children, and trading them for degrees and corporate paychecks. Half of the female population chose to go to college and rack themselves with student loan debt and/or chose to have children on their own and try to find an economically attractive man to rescue them. The other half of women aborted their children after obtaining degrees and jobs then planned on hitting a buzzer-beater as the clock winds down. Few women are choosing to cash in their most fertile years for men who are worth their salt to start stable families. As a result, the birthrate has continued to decline. Prior to 1970 (before feminism: here we go again), the average age of women giving birth to a child was age 21. Today, the average age is 28 and it is not out of the norm to see several 40-year-old women in delivery wards. This is an important point as we will be discussing Sexual Marketplace Value later in this book. We know what the window of fertility is for women, but women who bought into the feminism lie often find themselves on the other side of IVF needles when the window starts closing.

Everything changed at a particular point in history, ushered in by legislative changes aimed towards helping women. Increased childcare cost, single motherhood, college participation and graduation, women in the workplace and male disenfranchisement changed significantly. It wasn't just the economy. Feminism wants to take all of the credit for its achievement, but never the blame for its failures.

CAT FOOD AND POVERTY

Despite what feminism has told women, there isn't more money for strong, independent women. Single-person households tend to have the highest level of poverty. As women in single-person household age, so does their rate of poverty and the rates skyrocket after the age of 60. The likelihood increases significantly when there is a downturn in the economy or during times of war because women typically tie themselves to jobs and corporations that depend on a good economy. Single people in general, end up in more poverty far more than married people, but women are the most vulnerable.

HOW WE WILL LOOK AT FEMINISM IN 150 YEARS
    I'm never one to shy away from making bold statements and predictions. If you have followed my content on YouTube and Instagram, you will see that I have discussed topics about colleges and universities closing their doors and about how women will come to regret buying into the *Sex And The City* culture. Both of these examples would later be backed up by school closure the following school year and when the creator of SATC openly discussed regretting pursuing her career over having a family at 60 years old.

    But, this may be my boldest statement yet and I really believe this one. There is too much evidence to support the failed revolution of feminism to dispute it. Unfortunately, I may not be around to see this prediction come to fruition, but hopefully, my content and this book will be evidence that I was willing to make such a bold prediction about the future.

    I believe that in 150 years, we will view Feminism the same way we look at slavery today. How's that for boldness!?!

    Every generation has implemented a systematic program that at that particular time, was believed to be the best idea. Recent examples in history include the American slave trade, Prohibition, Stop and Frisk laws and Affirmative Action. In today's eyes, when we look at slavery, it simply doesn't make sense. It's inhumane, the result of it disenfranchised African-American people for centuries and I don't think black people have fully recovered from being bought and sold into forced labor.

However, there were people who defended the institution despite it being inhumane, barbaric and despite it forcing owners to support, feed and house up to three generations of slaves on their properties. But, because the economy of many states and cities was tied to cotton, tobacco and other commodities, people justified the system through the lens of their eyes of that day.

Now when we look at it today, it's easy to ask, "How could they do that to this group of people? Because our economy and emotions are no longer tied to slavery, we can't believe that people ever decided to participate in it.

When we look at feminism with today's eyes, it seems like a good idea because we're basically trying to empower a group of people that were previously discriminated against, in order for them to contribute to the economy. The more women that work, the more of them can be taxed and the less you have to financially support. A win-win for the government!

The problem is that what feminism has done is that it rallied around the empowerment of 100 women but only five of those 100 actually benefited from the movement. The other 95 were forced to fill a role that they didn't desire or they ended up in roles that they would've chosen anyway. Some chose to do absolutely nothing. As much as the five people were able to contribute in the form of resources and taxes, the other 95 people actually chose to accept support in the form of husbands, jobs with stagnant wages or government programs. In the process, it has marginalized 25 out of 100 men. It has put an additional 25 men behind the 8-ball and it has divorce-raped 50 men in the family court system. 75 men were taxed in order to support the 95 women that the government pledged support to, who weren't able to take advantage of the empowerment movement.

When you take our eyes and send them 150 years in the future, they're going to see the same thing we are saying today regarding slavery. Men chose to participate in a system that disenfranchised most of them and cost the government more than it was able to recoup from women.

When Kanye West said "slavery was a choice," he was highly misunderstood and shamed by those who based their life on their feelings. But, if you look closely, what he meant to say was "How can you allow yourself to be a slave?"

Today, men have accepted their fate and given in to the feminist ideology. They are sitting idly and watching feminism destroy the country via socialist programming and laws. Men haven't even flinched. They have chosen to be slaves.

Just as there were abolitionists that stood up on the behalf of slaves and risked their own lives and freedom in order to free others, I am speaking out against feminism, risking my reputation and freedom in order to free the minds of men who have accepted their fate. In 2020, men are so scared that they are allowing this step-by-step, decade-by-decade approach to female empowerment turn them into slaves of the P-sleeve. Many men can't walk off the plantation because of their addiction to it.

Just like slavery, there are people who are justifying the disenfranchising of men, the high suicidal rate of men, the fact that men face workplace danger far more than women and ignore the conditions that men live in. Men are twice as likely to be homeless than women, but we walk right past a man and don't think twice about the conditions that may have caused his plight. There are men getting pillaged in the family courtroom daily, yet they're still justifying why men should get married in today's culture.

PART

II

DIVIDE & CONQUER

CHAPTER

4

THE MARRIAGE WHEEL

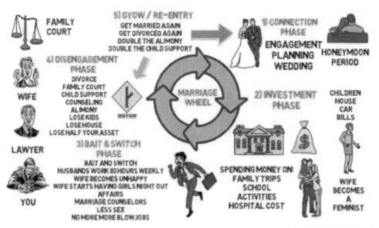

Illustrated by Alpha Male Guide

Feminism's most significant impact has been their attack on families and the traditional model of child-raising. It's made it difficult for women who want to be involved in marriage to stay dedicated to them. After the initial thrill of the wedding ceremony, women are presented with several tough choices and to be honest with you, some are bullied into choosing one over the other. Their self-worth is called into question and if they choose to follow the feminist model at any point, their escape route is incentivized through the family courts.

Women today want a wedding, but they don't want a marriage. She wants to be a bride, but she doesn't want to be a wife. The happiest day of her life is her wedding day. Every single day after that, it is presumed to be the husband's job to keep her happy. If he fails, his life will become less happy.

This happens to well over 50% of the marriages in our country and we know it's probably more like 80% if you include the remaining marriages which have chosen to stay together for a variety of other reasons.

CONNECTION PHASE

Every marriage enters the CONNECTION phase at 12:00 O'clock on the Marriage Wheel. This phase usually takes place in the first two years (YEARS 0-2) with the cost being minimal, although it will seem like a lot of money for young men. During this phase, each side has dated and vetted each other out as much as possible, they've met each other's family and spent, what they consider, a significant amount of time with each other. They have taken as many precautions as they need to vet the other person out. Here, the ultimate gift, an engagement ring is purchased to signify an emotional connection and a level of trust. They've committed to marry and join each other in marital bliss. This phase includes the wedding ceremony, the marriage license, wedding planners, photographers, florists, church and after wedding locations, dresses and tuxedos, bridesmaids & groomsmen and the minister/wedding official who will oversee the wedding ceremony. Don't forget the honeymoon. There is also the cost of bringing all of the family members and friends to celebrate this important stage of their life. This important transition into maturity, this rite of passage into adulthood, is what people call 'Manning up."

For men, what gets lost is that not only is he marrying her, he's also marrying the state. Although he doesn't realize it at the moment, that is going to become very important later in the wheel.

Some people get engaged and they get married right away, some wait six months and some can have a long-term engagement but this part of the wheel usually lasts within the first two years.

INVESTMENT STAGE

Now that all the manning up, doing the right thing and pomp and circumstance is all done, the couple enters into the INVESTMENT STAGE, 3:00 on the marriage wheel. This part of the wheel is represented by $$ because the expenses at this stage will dwarf the previous state. Both people will be making their most significant investments, usually with the female investing her body and time in order to reproduce and the male usually assuming the provider mode financially. This stage usually lasts between years 2 and 5 in most marriages. The family will expand during this time to include the husband, the wife then maybe one or two children, and with those children, there's probably going to be an investment into property, a house where the family can expand and create memories. In fact, one of these people is going to motivate the other to get a house and they will be emphatic about this purchase.

There's going to be investments in the birth and care of

the children. As such, there will be hospital bills, insurance, activities that your children are going to be involved in and education. Now, if they send their kids to a public school indoctrination camp, then it's going to be less money. But, if they send the children to a private school, which would give them a leg up in society, that's going to cost a little more money.

Family trips and vacations are going to be another expense, as well as visits to in-laws and attendance in summer camps and maybe a family pet. The couple is creating the picture of happiness and many of these memories will be shared on social media where everything will appear like the perfect fairy tale ending. The workhorse of the family, a.k.a, the provider has that goofy smile on his face in every staged family photo while imagining that he's going to have to work for the next 45 years in order to maintain this quality of life.

The ideal makeup of the family would have the provider working and the other parent raising the children. But, if both parents are working and participating in what Elizabeth Warren referred to in her book as the Two-Income Trap, there's going to be some problems later on in this marriage wheel.

BAIT & SWITCH PHASE

This phase is the one that catches every man off guard. Albert Einstein reportedly said "women marry men hoping they will change, and men marry women hoping they will not. So each is inevitably disappointed." Well, gentleman, change is here.

This point is represented by $$$ and usually occurs

anywhere between YEAR 5 and 12. This area is what I call the bait-and-switch phase. This is what happens when the wife decides to change the game. They're going to change all of the rules relative to what you agreed to in the Connection Phase. All of the hidden terms of the marital contract will appear in fine print in the new rules that the wife has now applied to your marriage.

For men who haven't placed specific expectations of what's supposed to happen in your marriage from year 0 to year 50, they're going to experience major problems when their wives change the game. This is specifically why "equal partnerships" are a disaster.

The wife is going to change for several reasons. One reason is that the real person is able to come out because the husband is invested heavily ($,$$,$$$) into the relationship. He's invested emotionally, invested financially and if he doesn't agree with his new terms, it's going to cost him more financially. It's going to cost him the house (that he was encouraged to purchase), it's going to cost him time with the children, the engagement rings, his reputation and all of the gifts and vacations. All of these things are going to go away if he doesn't agree with the new rules in the bait-and-switch phase.

Now, what has occurred in the phase to instigate the switch in the terms of the marriage? What happened is, a feminist appeared. Now, this feminist could have been already there or a friend or co-worker could have indoctrinated her, introducing her into claiming her "independence" or being a "real woman." If she doesn't have a job, she bends over backward for her man and family, she doesn't financially contribute to the family, she fixes her man a plate or she cooks dinner for him every night, some feminist is going to come into the marriage and "awaken her" OR the real feminist that she suppressed during the engagement and investment stage will appear, and the bait-and-switch will be initiated.

So what happens in the bait and switch? Most of the time the male starts closing in on his prime earning years. This is when his income is probably going to peak or grow considerably since the connection phase because he's been working his ass off in order to pay for a house, pay for his wife's happiness, take the kids to all those family trips, pay for private school, and all that stuff.

The wife may starts looking back and thinking, "holy crap I got married at age 25 or 30, I've had these children, I've been pregnant for probably five consecutive years now and I've been raising these kids for another five years and they're driving me crazy. I've missed out on my younger years because I got married in my prime and I wasn't allowed to be a young woman. I wasn't allowed to go out to the club and shake my ass because some man told me that I had to be at home barefoot and pregnant, cooking, cleaning and raising the kids. This is unfair, I got a raw deal. I want to start going to girls nights out, girls' trips to Las Vegas and Miami, because I need some time off away from my family and have some flirty fun with younger men and build my self-esteem up. My body is snapping back in place after having all of these kids and men are starting to notice." Well, it usually goes something like that.

She may take some action or measure that will signify her new goal of "independence" and it could be something that she knows the husband would not have agreed too prior to the marriage. This could be a dramatic hair cut, a change in hair color, a new nose ring, a new job, a new workout partner or gym membership, male friendship or enrolling in community college classes. Or she could ask the husband to make a significant change or sacrifice such as trading in his sports car for a minivan, putting his motorcycle in storage, firing his secretary, changing jobs, or asking for a raise at work.

A lot is changing during this time and biology is about to play the cruel plot twist game with her. The wall will start to close in on her and her level of natural attractiveness is decreasing by the day. The crow's feet come in, her face starts changing and the body starts changing due to birthing children and she needs to pump up her self-esteem. On the other hand, the husband's value is starting to increase, as more time at work is starting to pay off. He could be experiencing promotions, recognition and an increased raise in his status due to more income.

Another thing that could be happening is that she could be experiencing postpartum depression, dealing with bipolar disorder, having an identity crisis, or self-esteem issues, and as a result, her mentality is going to completely shift. She could be dealing with jealousy based on opposing career trajectories and may sabotage his ability to advance further by asking him to help around the house more, help with the kids, travel less or work fewer hours. If the husband is not pulling his weight financially, then this phase will be sped up significantly. Consequently, these issues will be compounded if she engages in drugs, alcohol, mommy wine times, picks up a new job and/or mandates that she attend girls' night out.

Sexual, emotional, and financial affairs start to enter the picture and these affairs can start to happen on both ends. The seven-year itch will hit hard and if the bedroom starts to get cold, he may seek another alternative to receive validation, especially if he's successful. At the same time, she's bored because she knows every move her husband is going to make in the first 15 minutes of every sexual act. If she's been reading any romance novels or Grey books, she'll start getting piping hot for any variety of male attention she can receive. It can be from the pool boy, a co-worker, young boys that she sees when she drops off the kids at water polo practice, her personal trainer, massage therapist, the dude bagging groceries or alpha males that she met at the bar or girls nights out. She may start to look at sex as a bargaining chip with her husband or something that she's only going to do on special occasions.

Financial affairs, which can be much more damaging than sexual affairs become prevalent. She's buying things that he doesn't know about and he's buying things that she doesn't know about. Emotional affairs start to occur with the dominance of cell phones and social media. This is when a spouse catches the other texting someone over and over again or contacting someone on Facebook or Instagram. If she's decided to go back to work and "contribute to the family" and "work on her career," either of them may engage in an emotional affair with someone of the opposite sex. These affairs rarely appear in the engagement or investment stage, especially for women, because she has way too much to lose by doing Monkey Double Backflips on a man with less status. Almost all of her financial, emotional or sexual affairs will occur at the bait-and-switch stage and beyond.

Once she returns to work, she's going to look back at the time in her Connection and Investment years as missed opportunities for fun in her younger years and missed years in establishing her "career." Some families believe that a dual-income household is needed and if so, she's going to have to get back to work. But when that happens, she's as much susceptible to affairs as the husband is.

So that's what happens in the bait-and-switch phase. The individual who he thought was his wife is not going to be his wife anymore. It's going to be another individual that he's negotiating with and probably someone who he would've never married to begin with. The bait-and-switch is going to cost a hell of a lot of money because he's about to lose everything if he doesn't comply with her new rules.

If conflict or resistance occurs in this stage (and it will), the marriage counselor will show up and this is the first sign that the marriage is unofficially over. If she goes to a marriage counselor and spins a tale and he can't get himself out of it, then eventually he's going to be directed into the most painful phase, the stage that he did not prepare for. I would tell most, if not all men, to just skip the marriage counselor and save time. The pain is coming, so get it over with sooner rather than later.

DETACHMENT PHASE

The detachment phase, also nicknamed the Divorce-Rape stage is when the husband discovers all the back end contractual terms related to the family law code that he agreed to when he signed his state's marital license agreement. He's going to get a lesson in law and he won't remember anyone telling him about this stage, despite the fact that over 70% of marriages will get to this point.

This $$$$ stage can happen anywhere between YEAR 5 and YEAR 18. He's going to start seeing the appearance of the following entities: family courts and judges, attorneys, therapists, mediators, the child support system, domestic violence courtrooms, potentially child protective services and anger management counselors. To make matters worse, these people will cost him thousands of dollars and all because the feminist showed up to the party. For men who marry feminists, especially those of advanced ages, these stages will show up all at once.

The family court is where the couple is going to fight over time with the children and the money that he's earned as he entered into his peak earning years. Today, many states presume 50/50 custody right off the bat and some situations may call for the husband to get full custody if he can prove that the mother has been criminal in intentionally restricting access to the children. However, if an attorney appears and convinces the mother that she can get majority custody or even full custody, then she will fight the father and restrict access to the children legally. She's going to fight him tooth and nail for the children and they will be the pawns for her to extract resources from the husband and THIS will drag out your family court experience. Most divorces occur after the Investment phase and this is why.

The appearance of therapists or the suggestion of therapists will appear not only for the husband but for the children. The child support system will show up and demand that he pays for the time he lost with his children. The time that he lost with them, he's going to have to pay for that because the kids are going to stay with mom and he's going to have to pay for her time with them.

Now, remember, the feminist showed up and said that she wanted to work on her "career," she wanted to go to a girls' night out and girls' trips and she wanted to have independence. Now, all of those things will become less important to her because she wants more time with the children and to focus on being a mom all of sudden. Also, without the husband fully financing her "freedom," she's either going to have to pay for it out of her "career" funds or from what remains of her child support and alimony. She's either not going to be able to afford to live that lifestyle or the husband is going to pay for her to afford that lifestyle.

GOING YOUR OWN WAY OR RE-ENTRY

From here, there are two ways a man can go. He can re-enter the marriage wheel and choose to repeat these same phases again with another woman. If he thinks that he just "picked a bad one," or "it was just her" he may decide to re-enter the marriage wheel within the first two years of his detachment. This is called INSANITY because he thinks that he can do the same thing and expect a different result. Statistically, his chances are minimal, but not impossible, as over 67% of second marriages and 74% of third marriages will have the same result as the first. He will find himself back on the wheel, with new children, experiencing the bait-and-switch again with double the pain. Worse still, he could potentially have two times everything else (alimony, child support, attorney's fees) with fewer resources to deal with.

On the other hand, instead of re-entering the Marriage Wheel, he can take that red pill line. One experience is all he needed and the distaste for this experience creates what people call "bitterness." But it's really an awakening! He goes on with his life deciding to focus on himself and enjoy it rather than risking it all on emotions. His friends and society will try to get him back on the plantation and when he doesn't comply, they will call him all kinds of names, from selfish to gay, from bitter to hurt, and from jaded to scared to commit. His decision to enjoy his life will be seen as a threat to everyone else who joined the Marriage Wheel, despite knowing that those people are likely in one of the last phases themselves.

If there are young children, the couple will never really be divorced. They will just live in separate homes and attempt to raise children separately. This creates an entire clusterf*ck for the kids and the parents, as the kids live out of suitcases and backpacks for the remainder of their childhood. As if that's not bad enough, there is more pain to come for the husband. If the wife has not re-entered the Marriage Wheel, she is more than likely going to use the children against him to extract more resources. Whether he goes his own way or re-enters the wheel, what's ahead is bankruptcy, financial ruin, financial displacement, potential loss of income, loss of a job or business. Potentially, he can become a criminal of the family court and face contempt charges because he can't keep up with excessive child support payments supporting two homes. The courts will give the ex-spouse the control to bring these difficulties into his life.

He is likely to experience more Family Court appearances and he's going to see more judges than he did during the divorce-raping. Don't think it's over. I've been to family court and have seen 60-year-old women coming in to file cases against men who owed back support from 20 years ago!

More counseling and therapists could enter the picture, for either the children or the co-parents which means more money.

So that's what happens on the Marriage Wheel and because we still condition young people to establish these relationships that are unfair and not balanced, the children from the original marriage will enter the marriage wheel themselves right around the time the husband finishes all of his divorce-raping. And the cycle will continue, especially if the children are products of a broken home or raised by a single mother. The evidence is that the marital rates and birth rates are declining in our country because most children today are the children of feminism. They are the results of divorce culture. They've seen their fathers, uncles, and grandfathers go through this exact same wheel over and over again and they're choosing to invest in themselves, their hobbies, and lifestyles in order to avoid the same traps that we chose to ignore.

This is what typically happens in 8 out of 10 marriages because we already know that over 50% of marriages go through this situation and end in divorce. But another 25% percent are starting the process each year but they just haven't hit all the spots yet.

CHAPTER
5

DIVORCE CULTURE

LOVE IN THE FIRST DEGREE

Fact: Fewer people are getting married than ever before. Despite how progressive women have become, the necessity to actually marry a woman has gone in the opposite of progression. The risks of getting married for men are too high, especially when the rewards are minimal. Since the divorce rate jumped from 25% in 1960 to over 50% today, men are more likely to have divorced parents AND divorced grandparents than they are to have both married. Witnessing their fathers, grandfathers and uncles lose financially has caused even the most hopeless romantic male to cuff his ball at the mere mention of exchanging nuptials. The truth is, the institution of marriage is dead and the vast majority of those that remain are on life support. This is not something I am celebrating, it's just something that is.

Of course, there are relationships that are thriving and I applaud them. Some people are making honest attempts at compromising for the greater good. However, even the slightest bit of feminism injected into a marriage or relationship can throw a monkey wrench into the program.

Even with the best intentions, people are struggling to keep marriages afloat, even though they were successful in their long-term relationships. How many times do we see couples that have been dating for five or more years finally tie the knot, only to give up on married life less than two years later? A good example of this would be Brad Pitt and Angelina Jolie. They had a seven-year engagement, but could only manage to squeak out a two-year marriage. Moreso, their post-marriage relationship looks like World War III in comparison to their successful long-term relationship. Add marriage to friendship and you lose both.

With the imbalances in the family court and the unrealistic expectations for men to be the traditional provider and take on the added responsibilities that the progressive woman cannot fulfill, it doesn't take much to send a marriage careening off of a cliff. Also, incentivizing women to leave marriages that no longer serve their purpose has started a mad dash of women filing divorce paperwork, and we aren't talking long-term marriages. 67% of the marriages that end never see their ninth anniversary, ending somewhere after the kids have entered elementary school. With the majority of divorces filed after the kids are born, they often become the pawns for women to use in order to capitalize on the cash and prizes waiting for them at the family court. It's almost a predatory act at this point and yet, when men elect to not participate, all they get are empty promises. Often times, the divorce is planned well before the wedding, leading many men to believe that there is some premeditation present.

"AND I'M TAKING THE KIDS WITH ME!"

We've already discussed the inequities and outright unfairness that men experience in the family court. With most states adopting No-Fault divorce in the late 1970s, divorce became easier and many women decided to leave their families and pursue freedom and careers. But, there was an incentive, a way for women to patch up any financial shortcomings that may prevent them from making it on their own. One incentive is to take the children away from fathers.

It is believed that 80% of modern divorces are filed by women. One way to lower the divorce rate overnight is to automatically award custody to the respondent and remove the incentive to file. A woman could cheat on her husband, initiate a divorce, be riding the cock carousel a week later, move one of her new boyfriends into the marital home, then collect financial resources from the husband for over a decade. It's a heinous system, however, I won't hold my breath on courts making this change.

When couples split up and there is a divorce rape impending, the children are affected. When this happens, the family court gets really busy and it's been maintaining its busy status for a long time because they have to figure out what to do with these children. When this happens, it creates chaos and the family court has to make a decision. When one of the parents believes that they're going to benefit financially by keeping more custody for themselves, it creates more chaos.

Many women seem to believe that they own the children; they believe that they can take them and move anywhere they want, choose schools and doctors without the input of the father.

The words that can ignite a full-scale WAR in the family

courts are: "...and I'm taking the children with me!" This phrase alone has resulted in a lot of bitter custody battles with both parents and children risking significant pain or damage as a result of this selfish act. This declaration of war dictates that one parent is going to use the children against the other parent in order to either capitalize financially via the family law codes or alienating the children from the other parent.

I often tell men, "When you hear these words, you have to make sure that you don't react emotionally because in many cases she can't do what she's saying that she will do." She believes that she has ownership of the children and because she's angry with him, she can punish him by taking the kids.

Men, you have legal protection. Most men don't feel like they can fight in the Family Court. That hasn't been the case in my experience and many judges are now trying their best to keep families unified. If you are proactive and you beat her to the punch or if you react swiftly and respond/file paperwork explaining her terroristic and narcissistic behaviors, you'll come out on top. You can't wait six or eight months because once the court sees that you've allowed it or didn't file any complaints, and the children are used to their new surroundings, it could put your case in jeopardy. They are going to do what is in the "best interest of the child." Then, the mother can bring in the fact that you only want custody to avoid paying child support.

When you hear these declarations of war, be as proactive as possible, don't be reactive. Run to the courthouse, file the paperwork stating that there is a separation and I am filing first so that you can request a 50/50 custodial arrangement. If she has already served you with the divorce paper and then hit you with "... and I'm taking the kids with me" or she gives you a photo of your kids and says "that'll be the last time you see your children," go respond immediately.

What you don't want to do is wait for her to do all of the talking, all of the filings and then move the child and now you're playing defense. Even if the courts say "NO" and you have entered your request with the courts, now you have proof that you made every attempt to be in your child's life, so when the mother is terrorizing you on social media, you have a legal record of all of your efforts.

If her backyard is dirty, this is where you capitalize and potentially get full custody. If you can prove she's alienating the children from you, if she violated the parenting agreement by moving without notifying you, has a history of substance abuse or she needs a 5150 evaluation, now you have a case to get full custody. However, you must be proactive and be willing to do the work. Just realize that men have parental rights in this country, you might lose something by going in there and fighting, but you want it established upfront that she has no ownership of the children. Both are the parents, that's how it should stay in the eyes of the law.

"I'M NOT HAPPY!'

Let's talk about those keywords that essentially light the fuse to the bomb that will explode your relationship.

Here's the deal, many times when women want to end a relationship they simply will not end it. They will look for your replacement in their list of friend-zoned men, beta male orbiters, friendly male co-workers, and alpha Chad's and Tyrone's while living under the protection model of their boyfriend or husband.

They will not be the dumper in the relationship and the reason why they chart this course is because this allows them the ability to play the victim when she is dumped. Anytime a male dumps a female, she can play the victim and say a lot of things went wrong and the reasons why they did is because of him. "He was cheating on me," "He was insecure with me because I worked too much or didn't work enough," "He was insecure with me going to girls' nights out or having a casual relationship with my male co-worker, so he came in and dumped me."

Many times women will create an environment of irrational behaviors and then wait for men to do the dumping. They end up doing a lot of things to instigate the ending of the relationship, therefore preserving her ability to portray herself as the victim and reap the benefits of society's pity for women who have "been hurt by men."

One of the signs to recognize that this disengagement strategy is in the works is for her to proclaim out of nowhere that she is "not happy." Now, many men have made the mistake in hearing these words and assumed that it is our job to make her happy. Men reflect back on areas that they may have failed and had even gone so far as to take accountability for failures that were not even his. Men have been conditioned to believe that it's their job to manage the emotions of women and have entered into relationships committing to the promise of filling her emotional cup. I have spent the last few years trying to break this conditioning of men who fall for this tactic and it is a very strong conditioning to break.

It is not men's job to make women happy in relationships and if she is looking to him as her source of happiness or emotional stability, there is a major problem! The problem that men in this situation face is that they've created a relationship standard not based on love, but based on conditions. They have a person that has attachment issues and the only reason that she is staying with that male is that he is meeting all of her conditions. Once she is no longer having her conditions met, she seeks to detach from him. She doesn't fall out of love, she is throwing a childlike tantrum that her male slave is no longer meeting her expectations.

Women with attachment issues are never single. She breaks up with somebody and ultimately she has a beta male orbiter or an alpha male that she had in her line of admirers that she can reach to and after a few days she's right back into some form of relationship. She's simply not comfortable with being single or alone.

It would appear as if she's highly desired on the sexual marketplace or that she's very good at relationships, but she's really in need of an attachment and she will position men strategically in her life who are willing to fill her emotional cup. It's not that she needs love or security, it's the attachment that's most important.

One of the brightest signs of recognizing if you are with someone who has an attachment issue is when something goes wrong in the relationship and the relationship ends. More often than not, she goes on the attack against you. If the person actually loved you, then they wouldn't attack you with so much hate and vigor. But, the person with an attachment issue essentially attacks you with hate once the relationship is over and it is because you didn't give her what she wanted.

For some reason in our hopeless romantic world, we believe that relationships are simple. Boy meets girl and everything falls into place. For women, they tend to believe that men who love them will be on a mission to please and complete them or are constantly trying to make them happy. On the men's side, we have this false belief that with our best efforts, we can build up happiness points or some sort of equity related to a woman's happiness. We give our best effort to make her happy one day, but those points don't carry over to the next day. If you don't cash in the points and take what you expect to be a fair trade for your efforts, then she will wake up the next day waiting to have you fulfill her next expectation. You're not going to get rewarded for the previous day's effort because those points don't carry over. She will have selective amnesia based on your performance and all of a sudden "what have you done for me lately?" is her motto.

The best approach for men is to get what you want first, then reward her for her performance.

She is under the impression that when she's not happy, it is her obligation to gaslight you or blow up the relationship altogether and seek another victim. By this point, she's already lining up someone else to fill your seat. She's looking to steal second base all while keeping her foot on first.

She's never going to break up or initiate a break up without her having another person in line and women always keep these men in line, men from the gym, co-workers and long-term friends that she told you to not worry about. These are the men that she has already got some sort of confirmation that they will be there, at least temporarily and they will appear as soon as the breakup is initiated or shortly before.

Unfortunately, in our pursuit of understanding what real relationships are, it is clear that we're not pursuing real relationships, we are pursuing attachments. 100 years ago, people got into relationships in order to survive, not based on the fantasy love and romantic partnerships that the Madison Avenue marketing departments created for us. People in the past came together for the purpose of procreation, to protect those children, to support them and each other as a family in order to build and provide better opportunities for those that we created. These are the reasons why we get into relationships. These are the reasons why we pursue sex. Women have that same desire, to procreate and protect and support those that they created. Today, the movies don't portray this, the media doesn't portray this. So, modern women today grow up believing that this is about love. They believe that somebody is supposed to be loving them and making them happy, catering for them, purchasing things for them and trying to entertain them. They believe men wake up thinking "I want to pay for somebody's date today! I want to love somebody today."

Trust me, most men don't wake up thinking about any of those things and the reality is most men only do these things in an effort to try to make a woman happy enough so she can lie on her back and spread her legs. Just like an investment account, his interest declines significantly after he makes his withdrawal.

The "I'm not happy" syndrome is just an excuse to monkey branch to her next victim. It isn't a call to action for men to correct their behavior. It is a threat or an ultimatum. Never take either seriously. When men hear those words, they shouldn't spring into action to make her happy. This isn't his job and it's actually an impossible mission. She should either seek help, seek friendships, seek a social group without that group being a bunch of sluts who are going to girls' night grinding on d*ck. Suggest that she seeks counseling because it is unfair for him to take the weight of her emotions or be manipulated emotionally. If she doesn't actually seek help, then you will see it clearly for what it is; an attempt to blow up the relationship and take your financial future and children with her.

Unfortunately, men who are addicted to the P-sleeve will never see this coming, because their next step is always how to get more P-sleeve. There are guys out there busting their butt every day on this hamster wheel trying to continue to make somebody happy that refuses to be satisfied. The minute you stop trying to make her happy, it's all your fault, she has permission to blow up the relationship and it's going to cost you everything.

Men must participate with women who have realistic expectations but unfortunately, they are few and far between. The chances of you finding one is slim to none, and slim just died.

WOMEN ARE DREAM KILLERS: SHE IS REPLACEABLE

Men have the infinite potential to create situations in their life that can change everything for them. They have the vision and the ability to plan. They have ambition and drive. They have PhDs but are poor, hungry, and driven. All of the things he needs to create revenue, to create the life that he wants to live whether it is somewhere in the mountains away from everybody or in a big comfortable mansion. Men have the opportunity to create something from nothing. That is our gift as men. Not only do we have the potential to do that, but we also do it on a daily basis. Day in and day out. Year after year. It is what men are expected to do. Sadly, it is constantly being undermined by feminism and those who suggest that they're equal to men. Surprisingly, those same people aren't willing to take the risks in order to receive rewards. They cherrypick the positives of masculinity (earning potential) and want these things given to them, without the risk, accountability, responsibility, and expectations of masculinity.

I want you guys to understand something. At some point, you're going to have a significant other in your life, maybe a marriage or potentially a finance or a girlfriend. You're going to have somebody in your life that's going to want a significant amount of attention from you. I've talked about this a lot in my first book, the Free Agent Lifestyle. If you are in that situation, a lot of times you might have an idea, a goal or dream that you want to accomplish and you're willing to take that person with you, so they can also reap the benefits of what you've created.

The sad reality is that many times, that person is not as supportive as you would want to believe. They may actually turn out to be "dream killers", people who want you to spend an inordinate amount of time with them and not have you spend the necessary time on your business, your goals or dreams. What appears to be support could end up being sabotage. They sabotage these things out of fear, lack of belief in your dream succeeding, fear that it's going to take attention away from them, fear that if you achieve this goal, they may lose out on you or that they may not be good enough for you when you reach that goal. So their self-sabotaging mechanism is designed to destroy the very thing you want in your life.

I recently saw an interview with Kevin O'Leary, an

entrepreneur that is featured on the television show *Shark Tank*. He talked about counseling a man that is at this point in his relationship. He has a fiancé, he's young and ambitious and he's created a great business opportunity that's generating a lot of revenue. Even Kevin O'Leary appeared interested in this particular business. It is one of those businesses that could change the world, not just the lifestyle of the person that created it. It could change the damn world!

His problem is he has a dream killer as a future spouse, but he doesn't know it. His fiancé wants him to spend time going to the Farmers Market, going to the festival, going to the fair, and going to family outings. All the big "F" words seem to come along with being in a relationship that always requires long amounts of time during the weekend. His initial thought is, in order to save his relationship with the fiancé, he may have to take away from his business interest, you know...the business idea that's going to change the world! He's considering taking time away from his business in order to save his relationship with his fiancé.

Now Kevin O'Leary in his logical, pragmatic and rational mind, gives him some of the greatest advice that every man should hear and that every young woman fear. He simply asked the guy "which one is easier to replace? A potential billion-dollar business or your fiancé? What is the likelihood that he's going to recreate a billion-dollar business vs. the likelihood that he could find another fiancé? The answer is easy, but many men choose the person and give up on their goals and aspirations only to see this person dispose of them years later on the marriage wheel. An opportunity missed!

When you get into a relationship with somebody that

potentially wants to kill your dream in order for them to benefit, you need to recognize that as a red flag. "You want me to spend time at family outings as opposed to committing time to my business?" "You want me to spend weekends at the fair, the festival, the Farmers Market, as opposed to working on these things that can change my life, as well as yours?"

This type of attention-seeking and lack of priorities is a major red flag. If you proceed with this particular woman, do you think her demands will become better or worse? If you marry her do you think that her expectations for you to attend commitments increase or decrease? Do you think that she will want to become more of a priority or less of a priority after you marry her?

These are the things that men need to consider. Most human beings are easily replaceable. Especially if you are in your 20's. There are going to be women that come along in your 30's and into your 40's that are going to be way better and more mature than the women that you're dealing with in your 20's. Follow your dreams and passions. Make that vision come to fruition. Would you rather be going to the festival every weekend or would you rather spend time promoting your business or making business calls? You only have time to create the opportunity that is ahead of you. Your priority is to create the best life that you can possibly create, right now!

DOMINANT WOMEN

Once men are invested in relationships, women have a tendency to want to dominate. This is one of the sh*t tests that I detailed in my first book, and this one is a giant sh*t test that even when passed, it will occasionally rear its ugly head again. My expectation for dominant women is similar to what soul singer James Brown said, "you must pay the cost to be the boss." And if that cost is not paid, by default you are not the boss, you are the submissive.

That is a principle of nature. In order to lead and be dominant, you must be willing to sacrifice and risk the most. You must be the provider and be willing to pay the price of that dominance. When the barbarian knocks at the gate, she must take the lead and she cannot defer. Once she defers, she can no longer be the dominant in any other aspect of the relationship.

SUBSERVIENT LANGUAGE THAT MEN USE
"HAPPY WIFE, HAPPY LIFE"

Let's talk about the subservient language that men use in relationships and marriages that ends up burying them and putting them in the submissive position. If they do it long enough, they will see their wife dry up like the Sahara Desert. There is nothing more cringe-worthy than a neutered male uttering the phrase "happy wife, happy life." It is downright embarrassing when I hear men use that phraseology, along with other phrases that prop up their partners in an effort to make them feel more useful in relationships where they otherwise aren't. Or, heaping credit onto their partners for emotional benefit.

To me, this is nothing more than an admission that marriages that last more than eight years are only successful when the wife is holding the proverbial gun to the husband's head. They know that if you've been married for longer than 10 years (depending on which state you live) if you get divorced you have to pay that woman for as long as she is breathing. Legally, she could dip into his pension, cause him to split the proceeds of their home, and split current and future assets right down the middle. So, the man is forced to make his wife happy, because he is a slave to her and her emotions.

For men who are going into their late forties and fifties, divorce is much harder to recover from. They call it the grey divorce.

Some of you guys reading this are in your 20's and have great relationships with your wife, but the dynamics of relationships often change as the couple grows older. All of a sudden going into your 40's, things became a little rocky and instead of correcting the ship, they anchor down and stick it out, knowing what it will cost them to jump ship. So they adopt subservient language in order to have smoother sailing. They stick it out because they know that most people, especially men who get divorced in their 50s never financially recover. They understand that unless they want to be homeless going into their 60's, they'll have to make this woman happy and be her dancing monkey until eternity.

It is better to pull the plug when these red flags start to appear in your 20's and 30's so you can recover and get your life back. You can get back on track within five years, should your ex-wife not use the family court as her refuge of revenge in the five years following the divorce. In your 40s you can enter into your peak earning years, get your lifestyle back and make a full recovery.

However, if you stick it out and things don't get better and you end up divorced at age 45-50, say hello to homelessness, living in an RV trailer or a studio apartment for the next 10 years. Or, worse, living with your adult children!

Many men are far too comfortable with using this type of subservient language which puts them in the beta male, servant position.

Other ways that husbands use subservient language in relationships is when they say things like "she's the smart one in the relationship," "she's the better half," "we can see where the kids got their looks from," "I'm the lucky one," or worse "my wife would kill me if..."

These are cute and charming and if said at the appropriate time, they would get a chuckle or two. But, we should be uncomfortable when any partner implies these things are occurring in their relationship. It is a cry for help and if they say them enough over time, anybody would believe it. That is by definition mental conditioning. If you hear that over and over again you're going to believe it. If you're constantly reinforcing this, she's going to feel like she's better than you.

Sadly, men do this to themselves. They accept the role of being the provider of happiness in their relationships, but the provision is extremely costly for those who do this in longer-term relationships. How many women do you know that are actually happy on a daily basis? Many of these same men haven't had sex with their wives in over two years, but "happy wife, happy life" right?

Even when men are the breadwinners in their own homes, they choose to use subservient language with their spouses and over time she loses respect for her husband, his guidance, and leadership.

Subservient language may appear to be words of affirmation or used to build a sense of pride, self-esteem or self-importance in the relationship when a wife chooses a role that doesn't get as much recognition as the husband. The husband may use these words to recognize the sacrifice that the wife is making for their family. I understand recognition, but I will never accept the subservient language as a means to deliver recognition. This is breaking down a man in order to build up a woman and this feeds into the entitlement syndrome of American women. This is male feminism.

"MY WIFE WON'T LET ME"/"I GOTTA ASK THE WIFE."

This is another phrase that is typically used when the wife is holding the purse strings in the marriage or controlling the finances. Men who are stuck in provider mode typically sacrifice doing things for their own entertainment or enjoyment in order to make those around him happy. When it is time for him to do something he enjoys, he can feel guilty about investing time away from his family. If the wife is overseeing (or controlling) the budget in the relationship, he might believe that he needs permission to participate in something for his own benefit. Thus, he is not able to make financial decisions on his own.

The crazy part of this subservient language is that statistically, in 65% of marital households the man is considered the breadwinner, yet still feels that he has to ask permission from the wife. They have to ask if they can use the funds that they've earned to do something recreational. This is a sign that there is controlling behavior on one side of the relationship and the wife is dictating to that husband when they can and cannot have fun, and she is using his own money to restrict his access to fun.

Ironically, tennis player Serena Williams recently started talking about financial abuse in relationships, which is the latest feminist buzzword that is sponsored by American corporations, specifically State Farm, to promote more propaganda. They are suggesting that women are victims of financial abuse in relationships and that men are preventing women from leaving marriages, despite the fact, the 90% of domestic violence shelters are female only and that the family court is a de-facto banking system for women who want to break up families. I'll talk more about that later.

In reality though, when you listen to men using this subservient language, it is the definition of financial abuse. Imagine if a woman was using this language in public settings: "I want to go to brunch with you girls, but my husband won't let me." All of the beta male orbiters and white knights would form like Voltron on a rescue mission. "I can't believe you're allowing your husband to do this to you" and "I would never do that to you, you deserve better my queen," doing their best effort to get into her wifely P-sleeve. Even if a woman addresses this situation with another woman, she would still be the victim of abuse and they would be attempting an intervention or to sneak her out of the house after the husband starts snoring.

2ND MARRIAGES: A FOOLISH BET

Second marriages are almost statistically perfect disasters. We've covered why first marriages don't perform well but the statistics of second and third marriages are downright scary, with somewhere between a 60-67% divorce rate on a second marriage and 70-80% on third marriages.

Second marriages typically deal with scenarios that the first marriage did not have to deal with and this is where couples are going to run into a multitude of problems. Typically, in second marriages, there are two sets of kids that are brought into the equation. If there aren't two sets, at least one of the parents is bringing children into the equation. Or, they can come from a single motherhood household. The expectation involved with second marriages is that you are most likely going to be raising someone else's child or at least be a part of their life.

If you get into a situation where you're going to be a primary parent to that child, the Stepfather, you're already entering into treacherous territory. I'm not going to get into every issue regarding this because it can be a book by itself. However, for every child that grows up saying that say they are glad a stepfather came into their lives and "stepped up," there are ten children that are never going to consider you a parent. The other situations are filled with kids proclaiming "you're not my daddy" putting men in the unenviable position of trying to be more a friend instead of a mature adult parent. The stepfather ends up trying to win them over with the little leverage that the biological parent allows. If both have children and both are on their second marriage there may be times where, due to split custodial time, one set of kids will be in the home while another set is with their father and vice versa. During times of overlap, this could lead to territorial squabbles and scenarios that will have you wanting to pull out what little remains of your hair. Of course, differences in the age of the children and parenting styles play another factor.

Many times men get into these types of relationships with children involved and may feel compelled to stay because of the child that is not even theirs. Here's another crazy scenario that I was presented with during a coaching call. What if your new wife has an older daughter and that daughter gets knocked up and has to live in your house with the new child. At a time where you may have been thinking about retirement, you now have a non-blood relative stepdaughter living in your house with her bastard child and the likelihood of her leaving the nest is slim to none. Now you have to raise a grandchild that is not even from your blood lineage.

This is why second marriages have a high divorce rate. People look at their first marriage and feel like it was the other person's fault when it ended and that a new person is an obvious solution. Of course, these relationships are going to be good at the beginning, but if she's already been divorced, she already knows how to pull the trigger and knows how to go down to the courthouse and make things difficult for you. If she's already pulled the trigger on one marriage, especially with children involved, she should be off-limits and shouldn't even be considered for marriage material. These are the things that you can inherit and it'll almost certainly fail, as opposed to it working.

CHAPTER
6

MEDIA PROPAGANDA MACHINE

One of the questions that I'm asked more often than I'd prefer is "What actions can men take to counteract feminism?" The questioner is often referring to a type of activism or protest in order to correct the issues that men face in this one-sided non-versation. They are disappointed when I suggest that proactive or reactive protests would be counterproductive. Men's Rights Activists have done a significant amount of the work at the turn of the century, even getting to the point of having women involved in their movement to add credibility.

It is debatable whether their advocacy made an impact; however, I will say that custody issues have gotten slightly better for men in some states since MRAs began highlighting parental rights issues.

Feminism has a more powerful shield to penetrate. They have the power to silence voices that oppose them. They have backing from college and university so-called professors who have campuses under siege in order to indoctrinate young minds while they're away from their parents. They have the support of local, state, and national government politicians and lobbyist groups that influence legislators. Most importantly, they have corporations that are compliant with the previous groups to use the media to influence the thought and behaviors of the public.

The only answer to the question is: Continue to talk about them. A lot! It works and they hate it. Feminists hate themselves and the proof is their penis envy. They want to co-opt every masculine trait that produces resources and discards the traits that require risk and accountability. When you show feminists their reflection, they can't accept the fact that nature gave them what they believe are inferior characteristics. When we talk, they don't rebut, they attempt to silence and intimidate. But, I've never seen a feminist defend themselves without emotions or account for their shortcomings. I've also never seen one back up a threat with force. So, keep talking about them. It exposes them and they HATE it!

GET WOKE, GO BROKE

When you have media in your back pocket spreading messages of so-called women's empowerment, your cause may appear unstoppable because it's running unopposed. They are able to produce content in "good faith" that you cannot get away from. Just watching a football game or sports highlight show will yield obvious agenda-driven stories and commercials that the viewer never asked for. The Effeminate Sports Programming Network has been guilty of pandering to underrepresented groups that may or may not have real buying power. It has resulted in them losing large subscription accounts of many men in their core audience when they already had a near-perfect product. When you insult the intelligence of your audience or browbeat them on political or racial issues in order to make them feel guilty, the viewer leaves. Sports were a place where men were looking to escape the madness and expectations the world placed on them. Now, the invaders of "truth" have taken sports and made it a vehicle for "social change" and "awareness" issues that they have carefully selected for us to care about.

The No Fun League had to resolve the Colin Kaepernick national anthem protest with tender loving care while a bunch of squirming sponsors and the mid-American fan base struggled to figure out whether they wanted to park their money for a cause they didn't want to support or oppose. But, the league had a difficult decision because as much as they didn't want a controversial social issue playing itself out on the field, they couldn't say that they didn't hold their viewers hostage with similar select causes that they supported. They had no problem embracing pink gloves and cleats on the field to drive home the need to raise funds for women suffering from breast cancer while ignoring men who suffer from prostate cancer, which affects more people. What about the commercial that paints men as initiators of Domestic Violence, when statistically, men are victims of domestic violence almost equally. A low-level female assistant coach for the San Francisco 49ers gets showcased for being the first openly gay female coach to be in the Super Bowl, but the league can never find time to highlight issues that affect men.

Professional Basketball also had to have their players tight-rope serious social issues, informing players to be careful highlighting police brutality and at the same time taking an odd no-nonsense stance against discriminatory laws related to transgender bathroom usage — in North Carolina. Haha, I mean, how many times is that really going to be an issue...in North Carolina? And, let's not forget the debacle that was the China/Hong Kong "debate" where the league got its hand dirty in real political issues and didn't like it. Many outspoken players and league officials who had been vocal on issues regarding women's empowerment and gender rights all of a sudden wanted to abdicate the political throne when their pockets were affected. True hypocrites through and through. The league is also pushing for women referees and are on the verge of hiring a female head coach when the league's all-time leading scorer Kareem Abdul-Jabbar couldn't even get a job.

The traditional media can't even be trusted as legit sources anymore. I mean, even after their stories continue to be debunked, they still report them as true years later, presenting data that is obviously false and running it unopposed. The endless stories about the so-called Gender Pay Gap are still reported as fact and even government officials like President Barack Obama claim them to be true when they have been proved to be false. I look forward to my future smear campaign after the release of this book.

Just when you think you can depend on commercials to give you a break from the madness, even those are filled with more propaganda. It is pretty common for commercials to make women look smarter and make men look like buffoons. Of course, since 85% of consumer spending in America is controlled by women, men's reputation and position in the social hierarchy are disposable and corporations will do anything to praise and uplift women to push them to the checkout stand, and that includes disposing of men.

Speaking of disposable, Gillette, the company that has sold razors almost exclusively to men for over 118 years, ran afoul of millions of men when they hired a feminist production company to create advertisements to attack - -

MEN! Their main customer base.

GILLETTE - THE BEST A SIMP CAN BE

In January 2019, Gillette released a commercial highlighting what they considered "Toxic Masculinity" in an advertisement campaigned titled The Best A Man Can Be. It was obviously an attack on masculinity and I believe that it was prepped to be run during the following month's "Big Football Game." Why Gillette would decide to destroy its company's reputation and attacked the primary purchaser of their supplies, razors, and shaving cream is beyond me. But, if I didn't know better, Gillette and/or their parent company Proctor and Gamble may have intentionally been trying to lower the value of the company to sell it off and get out of the razor business. With the popularity of men growing beards, choosing to shave less and displaying a more masculine look, maybe men were disposable to them. They started by hiring outspoken feminist producers that would come up with an advertisement campaign in which they would attempt to redefine masculinity.

This has been a common thing for companies to engage in, essentially complain about men, only to cry out for masculine men when men are needed to make significant sacrifices in order to protect them.

In the ad, they took everything that is supposedly masculine and destroyed it. They portrayed young boys roughhousing as a hostile act that "real" men should not. We should eliminate the "boys will be boys" mindset and have all boys sitting at the picnic table painting their fingernails. It was portrayed as bullying, which has been the new buzzword in PTA and elementary schools in the last ten years. But, obviously, we don't really understand what bullying is and we've allowed feminists to re-define it. While one person sees boys roughhousing as evil, others will find that it allows them to learn how to stand up for themselves. A young mom may be ready to step in and help her son on a play date, but must realize that unlike her privileged life as a young woman, young boys become young men that are eligible for selective services when they turn 18 and that skill set could be vital for their survival.

Currently, women are not even required by law to register for selective services, but even mentally challenged and physically challenged men are, in addition to the healthy ones.

The commercial also highlighted the #metoo / sexual harassment movement which, by the time the ad aired on YouTube, the #metoo movement had taken several bullets and many of their most outspoken supporters, specifically Asia Argento had begun to lose credibility with their own alleged sexual assault cases.

The advertisement also took issue with men pursuing women in seemingly normal social interactions and making them predatory. In one scene, a man discourages another man from approaching a woman that he was fond of and another scene turning friends at a pool party into creeps because he suggested a girl smile for a cell phone picture. All of a sudden, pursuing women is considered toxic masculinity. I'm curious, from the feminist perspective, how do they believe the world was populated? By men waiting for women to approach them? They offered no suggestion on how men were supposed to engage in these interactions.

They also showed a black father with his daughter in front of a bathroom mirror, shouting phrases of affirmation such as "I am strong," but at the same time, telling boys to calm down and be anything other than strong.

Many men logged onto the social media accounts in disgust to make their voice heard and most encouraged men to boycott not only Gillette's products but Procter & Gamble's as well. By the results of their YouTube video, which was significantly downvoted and peppered with negative reactions from men AND women, it appeared that Gillette might be willing to do an about-face and clear up their position. Some of the negative feedback was being deleted by someone managing their page, further demonstrating that the conversation between men and women is entirely one-sided. The comments from those who favored the advertisement's negative depiction of men were predictable, suggesting "that the men who have a problem with the commercial are the ones who need to change."

To further virtue signal, Gillette pledged to "donate $1,000,000 per year for the next three years to nonprofit organizations executing programs in the United States designed to inspire, educate and help men of all ages achieved their personal best and become role models for the next generation." Let me guess what organizations are going to benefit the most. It sounds like a transfer of wealth scheme to me.

For so long men have been protecting individuals who couldn't protect themselves in order to have a leveled playing field. Now, it's come to the point that men have to walk on eggshells just to protect these individuals' fragile egos.

Many of these egos have flocked to fields like media, entertainment, and psychology so they can protect themselves by using their influence to control the narrative. They've become prominent in media agencies so they can keep producing this propaganda.

Judging by the number of mothers who are willing to throw a dress and fingernail polish on their young boys at the slightest sign of effeminate actions, little boys need men and masculinity in their lives and less single mothers and feminists. Men have been thriving in masculinity for thousands of years but feminists have infiltrated the media and have given themselves the power to define masculinity, despite having never been men.

Sadly, men continued to talk about it and share the commercial with other men. They voted with their wallets and judging from future decisions their company made, the impact was swift and powerful.

GILLETTE BACK OUT OF SJW GAME

By August 2019, Gillette announced that they were getting out of the social justice warrior game after pretty much annihilating themselves in the market and to their fanbase. In an attempt to crawl back to men, they committed to creating a new campaign where they would highlight "heroic men." The problem was, it was #toolate for Gillette. Men continued to boycott their brand and voted with their wallets resulting in Proctor & Gamble reporting an $8 billion dollar right down and about $5.2 billion dollars net loss after the news about write down came out. After the arrogant refusal to pull the original ad, they would double down on their stance by revealing in March 2019 that the negative response "was all worth it," when anyone could clearly see that this was a case of "all attention is good attention" gone wrong. They even tripled down and posted an ad featuring a transgendered male learning how to shave for the first time. Boy!

Finally abandoning their position and finding out men weren't going to be the Best Male Feminists That They Could Be, Gillette would tuck tail and look to highlight men doing positive acts of courage. The "toxic masculinity" portrayal of men was not going to work and men finally stood up for themselves. To their credit, a small group of women said #NoThanks to the message that Gillette was trying to send. Gillette allegedly manipulated up and down votes and views after scores of people rejected their stance.

A lot of companies are going to continue to go through this pain. Based on feminism and affirmative action quotas, these companies filled their marketing offices with young women, who were eager to please the masses of progressive thinkers on their Twitter accounts. Now that they are in a prominent position, these young women want to hit a home run and create marketing ads to finally even the score and create the narrative that the "Future Is Female."

Many of these young women came fresh off of their college campuses and sorority homes believing that they knew how to sell to men. Then, they convinced these companies to jump on board of these emotional express campaigns and these are the results. The beta male managers who thought that handing over their billion-dollar marketing budgets to sorority girls was a good idea found out the hard way. These social justice warriors want those who they perceive to have the power to bow down just because they have an opinion. They want everything to be given to them, but the men who built companies like Gillette into billion-dollar businesses didn't operate on their emotions. It required hard work, effort, intelligent risk and properly dealing with consequences to make these companies thrive. Not browbeating their customer base with propaganda and morality issues, then arrogantly holding on to a failing position.

Companies like Netflix are going to experience some trouble as they are showcasing a lot of agenda-driven videos in front of their subscribers that they never asked for. Even when they report that they've lost millions of subscribers, they will never admit to why it is happening. The Sports Network finally woke up and got rid of all of their so-called political commentaries and then they pulled away from the features on Caitlyn Jenner and returned to focus on just sports. Movies in the Marvel Cinematic Universe, James Bond legacy, Ghostbusters, and Charlie's Angels will have to battle their way out of the agenda-driven movie business after trying to force-feed movies that feature women acting masculine or replacing the men who made the roles popular with women who could not carry the load.

It is clear that men with opinions are being silenced and censored because it doesn't fit the narrative and social media platforms like Facebook and YouTube have made it difficult for men that have a voice, in order to spin their narrative that women can win. But, IF women win, it will only happen when men have both hands tied behind their backs, blindfolded and gagged. They are silencing one side and allowing another voice to grow. That is not equality. That is suppression.

Many of these companies may find out that it's #toolate, as they double, triple and quadruple down on their pledge to attack masculinity. Continue to boycott these companies, do not buy any of their supplies and let them burn themselves. Men have real power, we have the ability to vote with our wallets, we don't have to protest or march, we don't have to put on pink pussy hats with little ears on them, our power is in our wallets. A lot of companies are feeling the pain right now and there are more companies to come.

SERENA WILLIAMS: FINANCIAL ABUSE?

In August 2019, Allstate would put money into one of their later feminist Hail Mary's when they hired tennis player Serena Williams to highlight domestic violence, the financial variety. The campaign suggested that women who suffer domestic violence may not be able to leave toxic relationships because men are financially abusing them. In essence, cutting off their access to money to keep them at home. Making them keep track of spending by "asking for receipts for every little thing that you purchase," "spending their paychecks," "cutting off access to the wive's bank account" or "taking credit cards out in the names of wives."

When I saw the commercial and started listening to what she was saying, the first thing that came to my mind was "are you kidding me?" Financial abuse in marriage can be easily proven by husbands who have wives that keep track of men's spending, with many husbands being guilted into not spending any money at all. Dating itself is financial abuse of men, in essence, if you aren't willing to pay, then you can't play.

What about the financial abuse of the legal system against men? They talked about men restricting women from working but left out the fact that men are often forced to stay in jobs that they don't like in order to support their families.

The process of going through a divorce is financial abuse in itself, with many men forced legally to produce every credit card statement, receipts and items purchased, report any gifts that they've received above a certain dollar amount over a two-year period and they use the evidence that he produced and set alimony and child support payments. In 93% of all cases, alimony is paid from men to women. Child Support Services and other government-sponsored programs that basically stick a gun in men's faces and extort money directly from the employer, many times limiting his access to a bank account in order to collect the funds. Then, the receiver can spend the money however they want, with no requirement to report how the money is spent. But, Serena is preaching more agenda-driven feminist propaganda that goes unopposed because men aren't able to talk. She doesn't talk about what the family court does to hundreds of men every single month. Is this not considered financial abuse?

This is irresponsible and one-sided advertising by Allstate. This is really about what women do to men with the sponsorship of the state and other corporations.

Many people are starting to recognize the signs of the propaganda and have chosen to not put their dollars with these companies. The Get Woke, Go Broke push back is real, but the propaganda machine will always find a new way to control the message and the people on the other side.

PART

III

CONSEQUENCES

CHAPTER

7

BLIND LEADING THE BLIND

Feminism has many side effects that the believer never fully accepts until it is way too late. Because women are given most of the characteristics that make them valuable upfront, careful consideration should be placed on decision making when they are young. This is because life has a cruel surprise for them.

Some of the early adopters of the ideology are no longer younger energy-filled women with a platform to speak from and don't have eyes on their young bodies to draw in listeners. They are older and invisible now, with many of them needing the care and support that they once shunned as an insult to their independence. We will talk about that much later.

Now that some of the early adopters of feminism are well into their 70's and 80's, maybe it's possible for them to shed some honest light on the real realities of choosing their ideology over traditionalism. There are a lot of women who have aged and figured out that the remarkable gift that they had as young fertile women is no longer translating into opportunities, cash, and prizes. Living the last 30-40 years of their lives had to be much different than the first 25 years. But who am I fooling? Expecting a feminist to reveal that they were wrong the entire time would be a pipe dream. Or would it?

THE SEX AND THE CITY EFFECT

The television show Sex And The City was a cultural phenomenon that brought in millions of viewers per episode, most of them women. The show was broadcast from 1998-2004 and ended with two movies with the same title. It featured a character named Carrie Bradshaw and chronicled the lives and mating habits of her and her three 30-something friends in Manhattan, New York. Since the show appeared on the premium cable network HBO, it contained stories about the glamorous life of pre-walled women who were all closing in on the end of their biological clocks, continuously riding the cock carousel until the sound of the buzzer.

Shows like Sex And The City and later, The Bachelor would change the way women saw and used their sexuality. I believe that it had a negative effect on modern relationships for a variety of reasons. We've all have seen at least some portions of these shows and I'm going to be honest with you, I've seen a lot more of this show than I care to admit. But, by no means am I an expert. Nevertheless, it allows me to describe some of the characters as best as I can and relate them to modern women today.

With millions of influenceable young women tuning in, this show would place the De-evolution of American women on full display, as the women on the show chose to shun traditional relationships and marriages in order to maintain their independence and freedom during their peak Sexual Marketplace Value. The party lifestyle, alcohol consumption, Sunday brunch Go-Girls commanded a lot of attention and for women who were around before social media, this was the way to get the attention of men. In their mind, the attention of men was endless and as soon as they've had enough fun, it would be just a matter of selecting from the many suitors in their lives to settle down and receive all the good results of a happy marriage. Sadly, what they didn't realize is that being the gatekeeper of sex doesn't necessarily make you the gatekeeper to relationships and the dark side of the show was when it came down to having successful relationships, all of them failed miserably. When the sun was high, all of that could be disguised because they had awesome careers and miles of attention. For modern women, they believe that that is the be-all and end-all until it's too late and the wall has approached. Now all of a sudden, these poor women are ready to offer at full price what they had given away freely to hundreds of men in the city.

The lead character, Carrie was an independent woman who had a career as a writer and was involved in a relationship with the older man, Mr. Big (Big Man on campus) who was two decades her senior. He had money and status but was pretty much emotionally unavailable to her for most of the series. He kept his distance, he lived a red-pilled life, he wasn't going to propose to her or cohabitate. He would use her and then put her back on the shelf. Big would end up marrying another woman and Carrie would get involved with another man, but she somehow found a way to accidentally slip on his married d*ck a few times or ten. During the series run on cable, the two would never marry, but to sell some tickets, the writer decided to marry the on-again, off-again couple right when her clock was going to run out. If we look at relationships today, life imitates art and this is the typical approach of many delusional women today. In real life, very few, if any men propose to these types of women. But, the women who view these shows see this as a possibility and waste years in their career, chasing men who could provide her with a lavish lifestyle, paying for her to travel while she can live in her little Manhattan apartment and not spend any of her money.

The next character that stood out, Samantha, was the cougar or MILF from the movie American Pie come to life. She portrayed a confident, sexually charged pre-menopausal woman who used the cock carousel as a bathtub toy. She's often found mating younger man and screwing dudes in the closet when nature called. She embraced her whore-ness like few women before her and didn't have a problem with the lifestyle that she lived. However, at some point, she'd done so many tricks on the carousel, that she realized that she didn't have any real value in the end. I believe a lot of her confidence was false bravado, false confidence and the only thing that she knew she offered was that P-sleeve and at the end of the day that's all she was able to give. If you look at the women today, they have tried to follow her example more than any other woman, save for Carrie, believing that they can maintain their psyche and their Sexual Marketplace Value (SMV), then miraculously be able to turn that into a traditional relationship. Well, for those that tried to follow Samantha's suit, they are finding out that it's simply not working out for them the way they intended. These leftover women are all over Tinder, Bumble and other mobile dating apps trying to turn 20 years on the cock carousel into a real traditional relationship and "looking for their soul mate." It doesn't work like that! It is not the natural order of things because a women's highest SMV is between their late teens into their early twenties. You can't go 20 years doing Monkey Double Backflips on every Johnson in the city and then expect men to pay for what she's been giving away for free. It doesn't work like that in real life and many women are finding that out the hard way. Many of the main viewers during the show's popularity are now in their late 30s to mid-fifties. We're seeing the real effects of this TV show and culture on the physique of today's single post-walled women. Unfortunately, the TV show didn't deal with the long term effects of living this particular lifestyle and we would see later that those who glorified this lifestyle would later change course and prioritize traditional relationships after it was way too late. The redhead had what looked to be the most miserable alpha window-beta male marriage possible. The last character was married as well, in a missionary marital intercourse kind of marriage, but was probably the most traditional of the group. The other girls didn't respect her or treat her like a real woman but the reality is, she had what every single one of those girls wanted in the end. She had the marriage, the husband and the kids and her situation was working, but what the other women tried to do was sabotage her good situation by encouraging her to be as debaucherous as them. She was the epitome of what they wanted but ironically, they sought to destroy what she had. We see this effect in today's culture; women with good relationships desiring to live the THOT life (See: Ayesha Curry) and post-walled cougars who spent their lives chasing emotionally unavailable men, still waiting for Mr. Big to run in for the rescue with stability and retirement plans. We are seeing the effects of this type of programming on American women. The truth is that once she's lived the stray alley cat lifestyle, she can no longer offer a man loyalty, honor, respect and traditionalism, the hallmarks that all real relationships need. That is the natural order of society that we've lived in since the beginning. The lifestyle portrayed in these television shows is not what society wants and not what society needs.

SATC REGRETS PURSUING A CAREER

Sex And The City writer Candace Bushnell, a 60-year-old divorced woman with no children, recently revealed something that I've predicted many feminists would say.

Despite being responsible for glamorizing the strong and independent lifestyles, sexual liberation and exciting careers of younger women to impressionable minds, Candace would admit that she's quite lonely without children and grandchildren in her life and regrets that she pursued her career over having a family. This is the shortsightedness that many women should understand before they adopt the career first, family last lifestyle.

After creating happy images of a fast lifestyle and having women eating it up, the reality of life alone after 50 has rarely been portrayed by feminist ideology. Women who are approaching their 50s and 60s today were the women who consumed these shows, and many even attempted to base their lives off the show. They are now seeing the real-life effects of following this Sex And The City philosophy. Unfortunately, they don't have the biological ability to change their course. That is a very important point to remember.

The idea that they can use their prime years experiencing sexual liberation while maintaining a wonderful career is a great concept. The problem is that the train ends for most around age 40-45 when their SMV tanks and they've hit their peak earning years. Any attempts to have a family at this point would be near impossible and living another 40 years alone or having conversations with cats is the realistic outcome.

Now at age 60, after aging out, flaming out a marriage and drinking the feminist kool-aid she says that she "regrets pursuing her career over having children." Sigh!

Of course, Candace is a millionaire eighteen times over so her grief is not quite the same as the "career women" who traded their fertility for a desk job pushing papers and pencils. The reality is, that even a millionaire career woman ends up lonely and miserable in the end and much of her money is spent trying to deny the realities of her declining SMV. She admitted to using lip fillers, injections and vagina rejuvenation laser surgery to pep up her declining value.

After all of her accomplishments and after all of her drive to attain status, here she is at age 60, realizing that she has nothing to offer a man. A self-admitted party girl in her twenties and thirties, who attempted marriage in 2012 to a ballet dancer, made a last-ditch effort to procreate near the end of her fertility window. She couldn't last seven years married and now she's dating men who are at the peak of their SMV and prime earning years. Ultimately, what she's finding out at age 60 is that even with the vaginal rejuvenation, botox, implants, and lip injection, she can no longer compete on the marketplace with the fresh crop of young girls that appear each year.

This is a cautionary tale and a story that plays out for nearly every feminist and this is evidence that even the people who propagandized the ideology end up with the short end of the stick.

I can only imagine the number of young women who were influenced by women like Candace, who moved to metropolitan areas, hoping to find friends that would become lifelong sisters, that would keep each other's secrets and who could ride the cock carousel right into a buzzer-beater marriage. Most of them now have to accept the realities of a vastly different marketplace and a life full of cat food and labia repairs. A life where men see no benefit in participating in relationships and even workplaces that are one-sided and dangerous to their survival. Clearly, the reality of this lifestyle was left out of the movie and the television show.

MEN ARE DROPPING OUT

With the landscape of unrealistic relationship expectations, unstable marriages, archaic family laws, toxic workplace environments, threatening college lifestyle and the invasion of male space, men are finding it hard to be productive throughout the day because of simple distractions from women.

Men are dropping out of many spaces because it is simply not safe to be around women, especially alone. Whether it's in gyms, universities, relationships, co-ed ride-share programs or corporate desk jobs, the risk of having to be involved with women in the #me-too era and the victimhood syndrome of women in general, men are opting to drop out of co-ed spaces. It's just too easy for someone to have a bad day and cost a man his ability to support himself.

Men face real and false allegations after bad breakups, on a Friday night at the college bar, during a consensual sexual relationship at the college dorm, initiating the conversation at the work coffee station, inside of the family court or staring too long at a woman's booty shorts in the gym. It's not just these places; men are dropping out of relationships because according to many men, "women are no longer women" and while they're too busy trying to be men, there are very few good reasons or benefits to engaging with them long-term.

College used to be a place for young minds to learn and share with each other, but young men are vulnerable targets of social justice warriors and so-call professors who are pushing the feminist ideology down their throats and identifying men as a privileged class that is out to rape the young girls on campus. These young vulnerable girls engage in sexually liberated lifestyles and binge drinking but if you happen to be near one while she's getting a train ran on her by the entire fraternity house, you can get an allegation lobbed in your direction. These allegations stay with men for their entire lives, even when they are proven to be false. College has become a rest haven for the victim mindset and it could be a disaster for young men. So, men are dropping out of college and they're finding other ways to learn and earn, preferring entrepreneurship, service-oriented professions, and trades & certifications in order to create safe spaces for them to earn.

They're also dropping out of gyms and workout clubs, choosing to do their training in home gyms that they put together. Big box gyms are a rest haven for women who seek attention and they are easy to identify. They come in with tight revealing yoga pants, thongs, short booty shorts and sports bras doing exercises that they could have done on the living room floor at home. They're also taking selfies and stomping around looking for even the slightest bit of attention to complain about on social media. I've even seen young girls in the gym making seductive Tik Tok videos, twerking on the treadmill, while smart men do their best to keep their eye away from the pseudo strip show. In order to avoid the traps of being called "creepy" for partaking in these women's attention-seeking performances, men are working out at home rather than putting up with this childish behavior.

Men are dropping out of watching traditional television programming, award shows, movies, and network news, preferring the control of streaming services like Netflix, Hulu, and YouTube where they can avoid most of the agenda-driven content that aims to portray them in a negative light. Unfortunately, some of these platforms are being infiltrated by feminists and social justice warriors and men may have to seek other platforms to be entertained.

What about consumerism? Men are dropping out of buying frivolous items especially from companies that are willing to take swipes at them in order to sell to women. Women makeup 85% of consumer purchases in the United States and save for a few of the large items that men tend to buy with discretionary income (boats, luxury vehicle) "women be shopping."

Men don't have a need for much and can survive off very little and usually can do without all the knick-knacks and small appliances that women will fill the house with. The other factor that motivated men to purchase things in the past was to get attention from women. Especially men that are in relationships where they are sent to buy the latest clutch bags, lingerie, bridal dresses, and jewelry/engagement rings to put a temporary smile on his women's face. As a result, jewelry companies are struggling and have taken their advertisements to couples that live alternative lifestyles or outright pushing women to take the initiative to buy their own jewelry or even propose to men. Stores like David's Bridal are shutting down because women aren't coming in droves to buy their dresses. The marriage rate is declining and those that do marry in major cities are usually older and choose to have less extravagant weddings. Restaurants are seeing a decreased amount of couples on dates during the weekend and more girl groups are dominating the scene. I'm sure the orders of appetizer-only platters or shared entrees are at an all-time high.

Even the ToysRUs and BabiesRUs brands collapsed due to slow sales and while some people pointed to the economy and online sales as the catalyst to the brand's decline, you have to be a fool to not acknowledge that the birth rate has recorded four consecutive declines in recent years. In fact, if you look at shopping malls, a vast majority of the stores cater to female clientele and with the exception of a few tech and clothiers, men don't have a major motivation to run to the mall to pick up products. It would be crazy to imagine all of the large shopping malls abandoned in the next decade but it's not out of the realm of possibility with stores like Sears and Kmart going belly up and large department stores like Macy's feeling the crunch.

The real estate industry and home buying markets have seen more colossal industrial apartment complexes popping up and less single-family homes being built. Sure, the economy and stagnant wages in many areas have made it difficult for men to purchase homes for their families, but there are fewer families that need single-family homes and more needs for apartments, especially those that have roommate-style layouts, with bedrooms on each side of the living area.

The red-pilled awakening of men has made an impact, but the significance of blue pill men becoming aware has changed the landscape significantly. They are starting to peel back from traditional dating and relationships and are holding on to their resources. This has resulted in a collapse of several industries, and the traditional model of life is looking riskier and less attractive.

The dangers of working with women, socializing, and having long term relationships have motivated men to vote with their wallets. Many men are no longer willing to write a blank check against somebody who is looking to cash in because some woman is having babies rabies after trading in her most fertile years for a corporate hot box and now wants to get married because her eggs are drying up like a bag of prunes. She then reaches for the closest beta and fleeces him in the family court five years later after a baby or two arrives.

There are more men starting small businesses and a few preferring to flip hamburgers at McDonald's rather than continue with corporate jobs. There are more men silently stacking away resources, buying cars for themselves and traveling on their own rather than getting into long-term relationships. The complaints that men are not willing to commit because they're scared are growing and yes, they are scared of losing everything, scared of losing the ability to support themselves and their offspring because a woman woke up on the wrong side of the bed that day.

Many of the allegations in workplaces end up unproven or settled behind closed doors legally, but still results in the male losing his income, position or status. Despite the disingenuous efforts of women like Facebook COO Sheryl

Sandberg, who are encouraging men to #LeanIn and continue to mentor women in closed-door meetings and lunch dates, men are saying "F*ck that sh*t" and adopting the Mike Pence rule. The scare tactics of "all you have to do is not harass women" fall on deaf ears because false allegations are real. The backlash of the feminist #MeToo Movement has been felt by women in many areas, yet they still act surprised that men are not willing to set themselves up to be the next victim. The consequence of women supporting the transfer of wealth scheme will be felt for a long time because men are treating women with indifference and mistrust. The dropping out effect is only going to get worse if feminism and stubborn women believe they will dangle out a little P-sleeve and wait for men to come crawling back. I encourage men to have long memories and to make feminists live with the results of their emotional movement that ended up revealing itself to be women with declining SMV's holding on to whatever they can as the realities of the next 40 years of conversations with cats become real. Men will find a way to thrive in the gig economy and have always found a way to survive. What's more, every time they do, it is the women that follow, waiting at the finish line to entice the winners.

CHAPTER

8

SEXUAL MARKETPLACE VALUE: THE STRUGGLE FOR MEN

If you wanted a summary of the next two chapters, here it is: Women get the first laugh, but men get the last laugh. Now that you're warmed up, let's get down to the facts.

One of the major issues that feminism has presented in our culture is the idea that we can take the natural order of mate selection and flip it on its head. The ideology is able to convince young women to do so, but often catches these women off guard when they have to confront the realities of a narrow fertility window and a dependency on beauty products, firming creams and botox injections to cover their declining beauty. Through media propaganda and shaming, even men have been targeted to feel guilty for being aroused sexually by younger women, preferring to accept the ideas of "40 is the new 25," the MILF identity and chasing after the low hanging fruit of the dating minefield, Cougars.

Middle-aged women find themselves trying to hit a buzzer-beater and settle for selecting a mate that they didn't vet properly or truly value in order to squeeze a few children out. Then, these so-called mothers toss their children to baby sitter clubs or to the public school indoctrination camps and return to their corporate cages so they don't lose their spot. If the man is lucky, he'll come out a little less divorce raped than the next one.

Long ago, nature provided us a template to copy in order for society and communities to thrive. Humans have maintained this order for 20,000 years. But, modern thought, and I use that term loosely, is to have women's value be placed later in their lives, another attempt to copy a quality that is successful for men.

If we use female athletes as an example, they usually hit their prime in the age ranges of 13-25. Sure there are some outliers like Serena and Venus Williams who inexplicably are able to push their peaks well into their mid 30's. But the vast majority of top female athletes begin to lose steam well before age 28, while male athletes might hit their peak around age 35 and some into their early 40's.

When we take that idea and consider the qualities that make the opposite sex attractive, we can see that the Sexual Marketplace is no different.

SEXUAL MARKETPLACE VALUE

Sexual Marketplace Value (SMV) is essentially a base-level evaluation of what a person has to offer another person of the opposite sex. The evaluation is preliminary or superficial in the natural because it plays to our natural biological urges. In street terms, this has been used to determine what "league" a person is in or to set a numerical value on a person's looks or other qualities that are deemed to be important. The SMV is not to be confused with the Relationship Marketplace Value, which we will not discuss in-depth here. The RMV is much less superficial and a high SMV does not necessarily translate into a high RMV.

One thing is for sure; feminist ideology, sexual liberation, increased divorce rates, and lower marital rates have thrown the sexual marketplace out of wack in the past ten years. Most people, in particular women, are "F*cking Out Of Their League" and this has caused a disruption in the mate selection process.

While a woman who is considered a "4" on the marketplace can reach her dating app and get banged out by a male with a "9" on the marketplace (because it's a slow night for him), a man cannot do the opposite. There is very little chance that a man who is a "4" on the scale can ever reach out to a female "9" for a quickie.

As a result, The female "4" now believes that she can achieve a male "9" on the relationship marketplace, but that rarely pans out for her. Yet, she still equates her value on the sexual marketplace at the "9" level (a.k.a., 49ers) and assumes the position of the legit female "9's." This alone has skewed that dating landscape considerably and left many potential matchups unable to link up in real balanced relationships.

Let's breakdown the most realistic sexual marketplace value based on what each sex has determined as valuable considering basic evolutionary needs.

THE HIGHEST POSSIBLE SMV FOR WOMEN: AGE 16-24

The group that I'm going to talk about first is the age group of 16 to 24, which is the age when young women are well into their most fertile years and probably where they are the most attractive. In regard to natural beauty, they're not going to get any more attractive than this stage. Just to be clear, I'm not talking about confidence and women discovering themselves or those that use Botox, lip injections, fillers, and breast implants to boost their SMV. Those artificial products are actually used to mimic this beauty standard, which are young women in this age group. This stage is when men are naturally biologically attracted to women, although beauty is always in the eye of the beholder. If we were to use the beauty and modeling industry as a gauge, we would see that the vast majority of models fall in this age group.

Now, for those who want to contend with me about this subject or want to get in their feelings and call me some sort of pervert or a guy who's trying to justify illegal relationships with younger girls under 18, do your own research. What most people don't realize is that the age of consent almost unanimously around the world is 16. It is not 18 as you were conditioned to believe in the media propaganda machine. Now there are some states in the United States that have the age of consent at 18, but the majority of the states, exactly 32 of them have the age of consent at age 16. In Canada and the United Kingdom, it is age 16. You can go around the world and primarily it is the age of 16. Don't take my word for it though, do your own research and you can find out for yourself.

Now, the d*ck police will have you believe that it is a shame for older men to even look at a woman who is younger than 25 years old. They attach moral stigma and standards to something that is very natural. Pump the brakes here and understand that most relationships prior to feminism and prior to modern society had an age gap, where a man would provide for a younger bride who was virtuous and preferably a virgin, that he could build a family with. So there was always an age gap where men were 8-15 years older than their bride.

Today, women now try to date in a similar age range

and select their own mates for emotional benefits, without their father's involvement and look at the divorce statistics as a result.

What sense does it make for a man in his forties and fifties to date and marry a woman in her 40's or 50's? It just doesn't make any sense! It never would make sense to do that except in modern times. So now, you have women that are on dating apps who want to settle down and get off the cock carousel and think "well, I'm 45 years old, so I'll go find another 40-45-year-old male to offload my high mileage body, debt and personal issues onto." That's not a fair trade, especially when there is an expectation for a trade of resources. If you are a high valued male you're not going to seriously date a woman who is 44 years old and you're in your forties. It doesn't make sense. You'd most likely prefer somebody who is a little more youthful and more willing to provide you something of benefit, like her youth and beauty.

Women in the age range of 16 to 24 years old are at the height of their SMV and it will never get any higher than this. At this age group, with ease, they are able to establish short-term or long-term relationships with high valued men. Men with money, status, professional athletes, rappers, and musicians will typically date or mate in this age range. You don't see rappers running around bragging about sleeping with 40-50-year-old women. They are usually dealing with girls in their late teens and women in their early 20s.

Something that you have to be cautious about with women in this age group is that once they hit college-age, this is when they're going to experiment. They are not going to develop their sexual gratification skills until later in life, however, men will still prefer them whether they are skilled or not. Some men will object at this point and suggest that older women are better lovers and I would agree with them if we are judging on a short-term basis. Of course, they're better lovers! They've been doing Monkey Double Backflips on the cock carousel for upwards of 15-30 years. They have a much higher body count and lower inhibitions, so of course, they're going to be better at it. But, men aren't selecting women based on her skill in the bed, they're selecting based on natural attraction.

If you go onto sites like Seeking Arrangements, strip clubs, massage parlors, and amateur porn sites, the vast majority of girls are between the ages of eighteen to twenty-four. Of course, you will have a few outliers for people who have fetishes, but they don't have much to sell since there is not a high demand for them.

Unfortunately, feminism has convinced the rest of society that these girls are off-limits, that they should not be starting families and that they should not be selecting mates. This is when our culture begins to implant them with IUDs and birth control, deliberately delaying their ability to have children in order to get degrees and chase careers and happiness. Ultimately, this will lead to being a mistake because they screwed off their most fertile years where they are at their peak sexual market place value. After they've squandered these years juggling fraternity boys' cocks and parading their bodies around on social media apps for the world to see, they start to do desperate things to make up for the deficiency in their life such as the absence of children, the absence of nurturing relationships and the absence of family. You'll start to see them do things that are desperate on platforms like Instagram and the dating platforms, Tinder and Bumble.

For the girls in this age range, if they provide something

that is of value to high-status men and cash in their chips early, they will become equally as valuable over time. They will be able to get benefits long into their thirties and forties as long as they don't try to divorce rape their husband in the process to collect cash and prizes. Unfortunately, the statistics show that 50-70% of them do just that; divorce rape their husband and fall back into the category of the other women who are trying to cash in on their declining assets to ignorant men. What this does is that it creates the bottleneck syndrome on the sexual market place of a divorced woman, single mothers and the fresh crop of 18-year-olds that enter the marketplace every June. Mix that in with the next age group for women and you have a flooded marketplace were the demand has decreased because of the ample supply.

For the young woman that follows my platform and my channels, what you need to understand is that you will be fed a lot of feminist ideology, you will be told to pursue your career, get your degree and you will achieve equality and happiness. That could be true, but there is a danger when you depend 100% on that ideology. What you will find is that you cannot recover that time back and find high valued men because, by the time you do, your value has decreased. You can find someone, but not very high on your list of expectations. You could be a statistical outlier and win the lottery by finding a man later in life that will accept you, however, this is the time to cash in because your value will not get any higher than this.

It should be noted that youth alone will not sustain a younger woman's SMV. For instance, depending on her lifestyle, she can give higher status men indicators that she's impulsive and not to be trusted. These traits can send her naturally attained SMV and RMV plummeting.

Examples of this would be significant weight gain, a child out of wedlock, tattoos, odd hairstyles or color, excessive piercings or modifications, high body count, a feminist mindset, multiple divorces, not ambitious, aggressive, masculine characteristics, financial liability, and/or unintelligent.

There will be a small percentage of men that will not mind one or two of these qualities, but again, these are outliers and more likely to not be considered high-status males.

Feminism encourages young women to do many of these things to themselves and expect high-status men to accept a sub-standard and quite frankly, damaged and defective woman. When men don't accept even one of these qualities, they are labeled as a shallow sexist, a misogynist woman-hater.

Men in the same age group? 16-24

Men in this similar age group experience something entirely different. This is perhaps the biggest mismatch of marketplace value that exists and this is why I call many of the relationships in the age group: the mismatch made in hell.

Although boys at this age group are able to procreate, they don't have the peak SMV of their counterparts. They have not developed the masculine characteristic that women expect of men which includes status, financial support capabilities, confidence, physical stature, etc. Young girls and boys around the ages of 16 will begin to date each other, but somewhere around the age of 18, the young women will begin to notice men that are little older, whether it is their freshman year on a college campus or when they take their first job. The men around them with higher status, more income, and more masculine qualities will typically be slightly older.

What boys at this age are going to experience is exactly what women experience when they hit their forties and into their fifties. You can basically swap the roles. As a young male, you are at the lowest point of your sexual market value, because you don't have the one thing that women are going to chase and this is status. When a male is 16 or 17, he doesn't have the ability to elevate any woman's status, except when a married woman in her mid 40's has a primal urge to jump a young man's bones after she drops her son off at water polo practice.

Of course, there are exceptions to the rule. If a young man at this age is able to show some athletic prowess or musical talent that could lead to money, scholarship, or attention, then he would be the exception to the rule in this case. Maybe he's physically bigger and has a chiseled physique, square jawline, facial hair and showing dominance on the field against young boys, then that status will allow him to get a lot more attention. The other exception would be if a male at this age had a characteristic that made him stand out more than the other males in his age. For instance, I went to a largely Black and Latino high school for one year and then my final three years, I attended a predominately white school. So I was one of the very few black kids my Sophomore-Senior year. The year that I was in school with mostly Black and Latino kids, I didn't get much attention. I didn't really stand out as much. Fast forward to the next year, all of a sudden I'm one of a few African-American kids and that characteristically stood out, therefore allowing me to have more access to some of the women who were comfortable with interracial dating. When you stand out in some way, you're able to elevate your status among the other boys in your age group.

Other than that, the rest of the young boys are going to experience a hell of a lot of frustration. They are going to be encountering the social conditioning that boys learn at this age regarding what boys should be doing to get young girls' attention. Things like being nice to them, listening to them, bringing them flowers, asking them out for ice cream, pulling out chairs and paying for dates even when they don't have much money to do so. This advice will come from parents, media, music, movies, and magazines. For boys who don't have status, doing these things is their only chance to get the attention of the girls with the extremely high SMV that have their hormones bursting. Unfortunately, this conditioning will lead to more disappointment and frustration.

The young girls with their high SMV gift will begin to have an open competition between the young boys and the men with status and this is going to make it a frustrating experience for the younger males. The same girls in their age group will begin to date college boys and when they enter college, the same girls are dating men with higher status, the campus drug dealer, the college quarterback or some of the Frat Boys on their campus. They may be dating older men or possibly selling themselves out to them on seeking arrangements.

So, these are the men's struggle years and the cruel twist is that they're probably going to be the horniest that they've ever been in their lives and they're going to be ready to shoot their shot anywhere they can. Not only that, as you age into your 30's and 40's, these women that you desired so much will be "off-limits" to you once again, as the d*ck police will call you a pervert and child molester for maintaining that desire for this group of women.

The status that is needed to move further up the SMV will not be available for most men for a long time and unlike their counterparts who were born with all of the highly sought out natural qualities, a man status will have to be earned. Except if you're the exception to the rule guy.

The dark side of this reality is that boys who experience the frustration of following the social dating standards (being the "nice guy") to get female attention will notice that their counterparts are being taken by the few high-status young men or the "bad guys." When these young boys can't compete or get access to these girls, they express their frustration, only to be labeled as Incels or losers and unfortunately may act out in ways that put other innocent people in harm's way. The reality is they just don't have much of a chance on the marketplace and they probably won't have a chance for a long time and they should be told that. Instead, they are told to try a lot of things that just won't work and these young boys begin to lose trust in people instead of making their number one priority building the best possible life for themselves.

The reality is that you don't have your own place, don't have money and when you lack money, you can't plan dates or have a car to pick up dates. They are battling a lot of deficiencies already and younger girls don't sit around waiting for men to obtain those things. Their clock is ticking towards midnight and selecting men that have those things becomes the priority.

The good thing is that over the horizon, these young men are going to see a change in the dynamics and there will be a switch on the marketplace and it will be more in their favor than against.

NEXT HIGHEST SMV - AGE 25-32, BUT IT'S DOWNHILL

The next age group that I'll discuss is women between age 25-32. This is the next highest position on the sexual marketplace and this is their last-ditch effort to skirt the dreadful consequence of swallowing the feminist kool-aid. At this point, some women never get it.

The average age that women get married in the United States is age 28. Judging by this, it is clear to me that after fiddling around in college and toiling around at the workplace for 4-5 years, the realities of doing that for the next 15-20 years while their eggs dry up like the Sahara Desert, doesn't look very promising.

The dating standards for women in this age group are going to be much higher than they were in their prime years. Younger women really don't know themselves and some have only basic standards that need to be met since they're actually learning about themselves. They're also learning from the men that they are dealing with, but they're still open-minded.

Some standards will be completely outlandish and these women will float around the marketplace for the few remaining years where they have the advantage, waiting for prince charming to show up.

During this time, men should be paying close attention to the actions of these women. In this group, we are talking about post-college women who have probably done plenty of monkey double backflips on the cock carousel while they were in college and after, however, they'd begin to go through some crazy adjustments in their lives. They are learning their careers, trying to find their way in life, some have moved out of their parent's home for the first time and are living alone or with a roommate. They're trying to decide if they're going to follow the feminist ideology or if they're going choose something more feminine. Ironically, this is the age group the goes on-and-on about being "strong and independent" the most, despite being saddled with loads of student loan, consumer debt, and being chained to a 9-5 desk more than any other age group.

The reality for them is that the cohort of "economically attractive" and available men is going to shrink significantly as higher status men have linked up with the more intelligent women who were ready to cash in on the high SMV. What once seemed like an endless pool of available men in and around their college campuses and after-hour spots, has now turned into a group of not so cool beta males and older men surrounding their cubicles in their "new and exciting" career. They aren't surrounded by the same amount of men that they were exposed to in the previous age group.

So this is when we see an increase in the number of women who enter the online dating apps to seek out the high-status men that they can match up with their list of standards. They flood the marketplace of Tinder and Bumble with sub-prime P-sleeve that they still believe commands top market price, but it is declining by the day. Because of the demands of their new career, they are starting to come home later and working longer hours to keep pace with the men. They're starting to have less energy to go out to the night clubs or bars, where men pick up younger women and the reality of a fresh crop of younger women entering the market place each year begins to make these hook-up joints less desirable. The high-status, level headed men have taken the women who cashed in their prime off the market and elevated their status and all that appears to be left are the bad boy hook up club and the men still following the social conditioning, a.k.a Mr. Nice Guy. Here they are in their Hillary Clinton jumpsuits believing that men are going to have an erection because she has a job and more degrees than a thermometer.

To compound this issue, this is when they see more and more of their friends cash out and get engaged or married to their prince charming, the good quality men that they assumed will always be on the marketplace and would be waiting for them once they establish their careers.

Instead of having their own wedding, they're getting drunk at their best friend's wedding and banging the DJ in the men's restroom. They are forever the bridesmaid and never the bride. Their Facebook and Instagram timelines are being flooded with photos and videos of traditional families enjoying the happiness of life with their children, the happiness that feminism promised they would have in office buildings climbing the corporate ladder.

As the 30s are approaching and the quality of men are no longer able to match the standards list, she begins "dating down" and feels like she's doing men a favor by just showing up. The reality of not having children is slowly becoming real as their fertility windows start to close and web searches about fertility clinics and treatments will begin to increase. They will yap about not having their time wasted and become increasingly frustrated with the dating options because those 6-foot tall, former NFL players are all gone or are selecting the younger version of themselves. Being a forever aunt is becoming real and their friends and younger siblings will begin to pop out kids, left and right. The only hope is that she can meet a man good enough to vet in a short period of time that could impregnate her and be willing to accept a career woman as wife material.

The number of men that she's going to do monkey double backflips on is going to double and possibly triple during the time. Their reputation for being a great night for random men on Tinder will bring men back enough times to dry the well. But as the notch count increases for these women, their place on the sexual marketplace decreases. They are good enough for a weekend romp, but when it comes to putting a ring on a highly skilled sexual performing woman, it just doesn't add up for men. Women in the age range could have an average of seven partners in a year and if you multiply that by the number of years on the sexual marketplace, that's over 50 men that have entered her body, minimum. The false confidence of having many sexual suitors will be confused with having high "relationship marketplace value." This creates a problem with locking someone down in long term relationships, but the good thing is she will get better and better in her ability to please men in the bedroom. So, there's always that.

The biological onset of the WALL will be undeniable. In terms of natural beauty, the biological wall is undefeated. The body that young women have at age 21 is no longer the same at age 29. The wear and tear of the cock carousel and bar hopping will become more evident. The weight gain will almost be uncontrollable as the body makes its last-ditch effort to prepare for motherhood. The long work hours and the stress of their career will start to take a toll on them physically and all of these things will lower her SMV before she gets to the date. The lack of time that she has available to provide a high-status man with feminine qualities will lower her SMV even further.

The drive to have children at this point will be driven by a selfish need to achieve their biological imperative rather than for building a family and supporting a husband. There will be a little onset of desperation as they approach the end of this age range and the consideration to lower their standard list even further will appear, so instead of a 6ft2", former NFL player, maybe a 6ft regular guy with a job will do.

Of course, with any explanation, there is always going to be an exception to the rule. When I speak about these topics, inevitably someone will say, "well, my friend at age 48, who works in marketing had two healthy children and met a good beta boy that's never been divorced and loves her marketing job," or "I don't have to rush, I work 12 hours a day and I'm still able to date and I got plenty of good men lined up outside my door."

Yes, once again, that's called being the statistical outlier and being the exception to the rule doesn't defeat the rule for everyone else.

The feminist ideology is much to blame for this condition today. The egg freezing, the Tinder cock carousel riding, the delayed child-rearing, and Hail Mary marriages have already had a negative consequence on the declining birth rate and the divorce rate in our country. This fight against nature is counterproductive as a whole.

Men in the same age group: This Is Purgatory

For men, I'm going combine two age groups into one and the reason why I'm going to squeeze them together is that a lot of the decisions that men are going to make are dictated by their pursuit of the P-sleeve. Unlike women who can elevate their status through relationships, men in the age group of 25 to 40 are usually trying to get on their feet and basically, the struggle is going to continue for most. Some of the issues that they already have with women will be extended to this age range simply because the majority of men are still working toward their prime years.

The biggest hang-up is that men will still be easily manipulated by women and societies "nice guy" conditioning. Men are going to make decisions purely based on the P-sleeve and women in his age group (age 25-32) are in their mid-level prime and still maintain a slight advantage over men in the marketplace. Women will still dictate the terms of marriage, sexual relationships, and long-term relationships. Men generally are going to make critical decisions in their life based on the availability of women. Schools, bars, nightclubs, and job selection are a few examples. In that instance, women still have a little bit more control over men than they should.

Men who don't allow P-sleeve to govern and control them will be able to focus on their purpose and that will allow them to ascend to a higher value much earlier. For others, women in this age group will be a major distraction in their lives. Men will spend time and energy trying to figure women out, leading them on an endless search for answers online, wondering why women are so confusing and complex. But, the reality is, they're not. I've been giving men the answer about the reality of women for quite some time now. Men just won't accept it. They are still looking at them through the lens of what society tells them, more of that social conditioning at play. The "sugar and spice and everything nice" and "all you have to do is make them happy and everything's going to be fine," imagery will be hard to break for men.

My advice hits much harder and some men just won't accept it. "They are not to be pleased," "Don't argue with women," "Don't try to make them happy," "Don't allow them to emotionally manipulate you" are all things that have worked for men who are the most successful with women. Once men have that figured out, they will be able to filter out the junk and get past many issues that the majority of men in this age group are not able to get around. The time that men spend on women never equates to the results that women deliver and men in the age group end up wasting hours of their lives on a wild goose chase that some women enjoy to send them on, all the while doing Monkey Double Backflips on the man that they really want. That time would have been better spent investing in themselves and once they achieve higher status, the by-product of that is attention from women.

A good percentage of men in this age group will get married during this time and oftentimes social conditioning will motivate them to do the right thing or the ole "make an honest woman out of her." Female nature, hypergamy and the potential for bait and switch are super high because the women in this age group will be starting to approach the wall.

Now, it would seem like a fair trade for a 28-year-old man and a twenty-eight-year-old woman to join together and make the best out of an age-appropriate relationship. For the woman, it is smart of her to cash in at this time because she's living on borrowed time biologically and it is almost buzzer-beater time for her to beat that clock. For the man, it could be a mistake to marry a woman in that age group. Why? Because he hasn't hit his prime yet. He hasn't even hit his stride yet. He probably hasn't had many sexual experiences yet and now he's allowing one individual with a declining SMV to monopolize his sexual activity and as such, will control and manipulate him with ease.

If he gets married in this age group, no doubt he will have some good years and fun times will be shared and a family unit can be created if everyone focuses their attention on the family first. However, statistics show us that more than half of these marriages will fail and if you count the marriages that stay because of the kids, religious background and those that have to survive through sexless marriages or disrespectful spouses, nearly all of them will fail. Worse still, if they fail, there are a lot of bad years to follow and it will take a lot of determination to get back into a position to enjoy his peak marketplace value. Some guys will make it work and still be married which is good news for them. However, for the vast majority of men who don't make it, it's going to bring a lot of hell financially, emotionally and some tough times with their children. Most men will never recover from this hell! So he's really rolling the dice at this age and he must remember that he hasn't even hit his prime earning years yet. The men who marry here hit their peak earning years with their wives and over half of them get divorced at the height of their earning years causing a massive displacement in their lives.

If a man has remained single or has been sent back into the marketplace, the available women at this age consist of post-wall aged women, divorcees, feminists, workaholics, alcoholics, overweight women, narcissists, a lot of women with unrealistic standards, single mothers, women who've banged 200+ men, women with a history of STD's after riding the cock carousel for 10+ years, bi-polar/cluster B personality disorders and the occasional diamond-in-the-rough. It's like visiting an insane asylum!

At that age, if men don't find their true purpose, they'll be floating around allowing women to control them while losing as much time on the marketplace as their counterpart. The men who are focused and discover their purpose at this time and get on it early will be the individuals that can get out of this Purgatory a lot faster.

At the tail end of this age group, once men start approaching age 40, they could lose their mojo, their sexual drive or even their function. If you have a decrease in testosterone, have master-bated aggressively, watch too much porn, did drugs or smoked, gained a lot of weight or battled depression this may cause men to lose their ability to blow some woman's back out. Fortunately, there are ways to correct that but during this time in Purgatory, he needs to keep up with his body, incorporate squats and deadlifts to get those testes producing more testosterone, eat healthily and cut out smoking, drug, and alcohol because these may contribute to his demise when he gets into his peak years. On the horizon, if he's taken great care of himself, his life will begin to resemble the life that women had at age 16 to 24. Remember, when I said, "women laugh first, but men get the last laugh." That is over the horizon. This is how it works. It works in reverse.

Men will start earning more money than they've ever earned. Their status will start to increase. They'll be able to have more money, buy property, cars and all of these things that can get attention from women. Even with physical deficiencies, women looking to trade up will be willing to overlook if money and status exist.

Of course, we don't want that to be the case. This is when men see a lot of the women that they didn't have a chance within their earlier years, show interest after they've found themselves back on the marketplace after a divorce or about as a single mother. This is how the Sexual Market Place works. The women who avoided men laughed at them, shamed them and didn't give them a chance will start looking at them through a different lens because they're completely transformed men.

CHAPTER

9

SEXUAL MARKETPLACE VALUE: WALL IS UNDEFEATED

If you are a young man reading this book, many of the things that you'll read may seem impossible based on your current SMV. If you're a woman reading this book, this will either be a wake-up call or result in your room resembling a scene from the Exorcist. The important thing to note here is that the impact of feminism will seek to influence men to change what they naturally desire to do for what is socially acceptable. However, high-status men don't determine their actions based on shame from people that will benefit from his compliance. Men follow what is right. So without further ado, let's continue with the second part of the sexual marketplace breakdown.

WOMEN AGE 33-44: THE CLOCK STRIKES MIDNIGHT

For single women who have been in the market place for at least 15 to 20 years, your time is about to expire. Women who have never been married by age 32 will probably never get married. If they find themselves single, either they have been single the entire time or they have volunteered themselves right back onto the marketplace by either getting out of a long-term relationship or divorce raping their husband. What you have to question at this point is if somebody has been on the market place since the age of 16 when they've had the advantage in the sexual marketplace, why are they still available? Why is it that they've been able to filter offers, good or bad, since a prime age all the way into this age and still have no available men? Either their judgment is poor or there are no available men in their area. I'm going to go with the first rather than the second. Did they make poor decisions along the way? Did they waste a lot of time on the cock carousel or did they waste a lot of time having poor judgment in men? This is a character flaw and should be an immediate red flag and most women in the age group will have more red flags than a Chinese parade.

Women who sold their fertility to corporations in order to collect paychecks and made a conscious decision to not start families will dominate the marketplace. As the clock strikes midnight, these women will rush to online dating apps in pursuit of men who might consider starting a family with them. Despite the fact that it is more common for 40-year-olds to have children than any other age of woman, this is not natural and it certainly is dangerous... for the child.

For men who choose from this pool of women, say hello to In Vitro Fertilization (IVF). You may spend lots of time jacking off into Petri dishes in order to create your little Mini-me's. I mean, come on? Women have had ample time to find available men and have received plenty of warning signs that their prime fertility window is closing or already closed. Women will become angry at their gynecologist and fertility specialist, and then will be mad at God for dealing them such a sexist hand. The truth is, everybody should understand this by now, but there are people who are normalizing women having children in their late 30s and into their 40's. This will soon be the norm. Unfortunately, people want to believe in the feminist ideology, using up their fertility sitting at a desk job until their mid-30s when they're forced to try to find somebody, ANYBODY to have a child with. This is unfair to the child and its potential health.

For men who encounter women like this, I tell them to take a step back and don't accept the pressure being put put onto them. Because it is highly likely that you will see the same woman lingering on the marketplace for the next six months or even two years without any serious offers. There's a 95% chance that they will still be on the market because no one will be willing to write a check against everything they've worked hard for in order to settle for a woman in his age group. I'm not saying that all women are bad in this age group; there are probably some decent looking women. But, in terms of settling down with one and making a commitment, it just doesn't add up. Men often find out that the sex that she used to lure him in has all but dried up within 5-7 years. Also, menopause is right around the corner and the official dry season will be the norm.

Then there's this, and this is something that is kind of unspoken about what we're talking about women in this age group and that is in their drive to maintain their independence. They'll get really comfortable with the way they live. They do what they want to do when they want to do it. They're used to living without the counsel of men for the last 10 or 15 years and biologically women will lose their feminine characteristics and will adopt more masculine traits during these years. A lot of these things are done to get positions in their career fields. So, the most feminine women potentially are going to be in the younger age groups. The more they age, the less feminine qualities they may have and the more masculine traits they will adopt, especially if they were born into feminism. They do this for their own protection and survival as well, because if they've been living alone, appearing stronger and more masculine would be essential for survival. If they've had kids or are on the second round on the marriage wheel, you may see a little more femininity however the red flag in that is that they've already been through a divorce and they know how to pull the plug easily since 80% of divorces are filed by women.

The last point that I want to make regarding this age group is if they have never been married, The Alpha F*cks, Beta Bucks scenario will likely play itself out. These women would have gone through the carousel and will have banged plenty of Chads and Tyrones and in their pursuit to beat the clock, they will sync up and select men with beta qualities and a hopeless romantic mindset and they will use that beta to procreate with. Then once the IVF children come along, it is going to be difficult for her to maintain a relationship with the beta because she really didn't like the beta past her need phase. She'll be ready to return to work, pawn the children off to babysitters, nannies and the public school indoctrination camp and then she'll try to dispose of the beta and raise the child on her own as a superhero single mother. If the beta sticks around, it's normally one of these roommate, sexless marriages situations and the beta gets used for his provision. And betas are targeted because their hopeless romantic nature makes them believe that they are winning when a post-wall woman selects him. They feel like they put in the work, pulled out chairs, bought drinks, paid for dinner dates, let her cry on his shoulder when all the bad boys were running through her and his persistence and patience finally paid off. Then all of a sudden, when she saw the clock ticking down, she selected the beta from her pool of remaining orbiters and he thought it was his good-guy qualities that earned him this leftover P-sleeve.

The baby will arrive and all appears well. Then two, three or four years down the road, she's ready to go back to girls' nights out, on what will be her last-ditch effort to chase the last available Chads or Tyrones or she's on Tinder hooking up with 25-year-old men. Sooner or later, the beta is out. Usually, I would continue with the series and discuss women in the age group of 45 and up, but it is pointless because the game is over for them at this particular point if they are single. In terms of SMV, they are invisible during the day and a place for temporary comfort at night. Again, there are some attractive 40+-year-old women out there but for a long-term relationship, a marriage or having children, there's no point in explaining their lack of SMV. There is very little left for them to offer and for men looking for short term, non-monogamous sport sex, engaging with her will teach you a lot of lessons. The truth is she is reaping more benefits from the relationship than a man would at any age.

Men in the same age group: This is your super bowl

The struggle for most men is usually over around this age, if they have prioritized themselves above all, kept their body and mind healthy and made solid financial decisions.

For men who had to buckle up in their early teens and early twenties and then wander around in purgatory between their mid-20s until their 40s, their biggest advantage on the sexual marketplace will be experienced here.

Men have to work hard for and earn their position on the sexual marketplace and it takes focus, discipline, and patience to reach this point unscarred. I once heard it put like this: Women are born with $100 and get poorer while men are born with nothing and earn their $100. Something fascinating happens around this time. Whether the man is married or unmarried, the position on the sexual marketplace switches, where men with status and experience are more desirable and women in the same age group become less desirable and have lost significant value. The funny thing is, not many people truly notice or accept this reality and some men still find themselves trying to date and please older women who believe that they have still maintained a high-status.

The years from 41 and up will be fantastic! You might have less sex drive than you did in your teens and 20's or you could be a horny old goat. However, this will work to your advantage because, you're going to be smarter and in most cases, the big head will outthink the little head. The men in the Purgatory years who allowed their emotions and sex drive to get them into marriages, out-of-wedlock pregnancy or sexual relationships that were controlled by emotions are not as attractive once they hit their 40's. He's a rational logical thinker and again, if he's taken care of his body, maintained his weight, hasn't abused drugs and/or alcohol and hasn't had depression issues dealing with relationships during his buckle up years, he's on his way to ascending to status and more income. And, that gives him options.

Men can actually go backward at this particular age and date women who are in their prime or that are in their second stage which I called the next best available years.

Of course, women in his age group will scoff at men who do this and they might suggest that he's a pervert, robbing the cradle or dating someone his daughter's age. They may suggest "What young girl would want an old man anyway?" And never stop to consider asking themselves "What old man would want an old woman?"

According to an article in the New York Times that was published last year, it says for online daters, women peak at age 18, while men peak at age 50. Everything that I talked about in the chapter is backed up in this article.

Once a man hits his forties he can continue to earn more money in his business and career, while probably having less financial obligations. Men at this age may now be off of child support, alimony and have sent their children from their previous marriage to college and adulthood. If he's never been married, he should have amassed a good portion of wealth, created a business and capitalized on the free time that he's had. He has the advantage of the big head now outthinking the little head and the ability to focus 100% on his purpose and income.

The peak earning potential for a woman in this age group is likely behind her or on the decline and thus, the strong and independent cock carousel, twice-divorced single mother has probably hit the glass ceiling. Not only in her "career," but on the sexual marketplace. On average, their income peaks around age 35 and it starts to plateau and dips around age 40, which is ironically the age where women want to "quit their fun" and start something serious. The dating apps will be flooded with women in this age group who still believe they have an advantage because they have a P-sleeve, but their scarcity mindset and willingness to latch on to the first man who displays gentleman qualities and gives them a long-term commitment determines who actually has the real advantage.

What I just explained is backed up by science and social scientists. You can find all of this information in economic literature and government statistic websites online. Know this; those who are governed by their feelings and disregard facts, like social justice warriors and hopeless romantics, want to control the narrative with their emotions and silence those who are being logical and realistic.

Women in this age group will try to circumvent the wall by artificially inflating their SMV. They will initiate Botox, breast implants, hair dye and display girlish lifestyles on social media. 90% of women in this age group could not guarantee the birth of a healthy child. Some men unwittingly elevate these women's SMV by paying off their debt and surgery bills. They'll even suggest that men hit the wall because they are balding or have grey hair, but many women find those features more attractive, especially if a man is able to show status at the same time.

Biologically, men are still are able to impregnate women and start families, if they haven't had a vasectomy and even if they have, they can get it reversed. So, when people ask "do men hit the wall, too?" Physically they could hit the wall; however, the wall has always been linked to the ability to have children; it is not just what a person looks like physically.

In essence, men in their teens, are what women are in their 40's. They are both essentially invisible to their counterparts. If you take care of your health and finances, this is where you're going to have the most fun and the most success in the Sexual Marketplace. Unless you were in the 20% of high-status men in your mid 20's and early 30's.

For those men who have let themselves go and have given up or maybe experienced depression because of the struggle years on the sexual marketplace or even a divorce, then and only then can you say a man has hit the wall. If they were trying to date and have not found success in the age group, they may have taken themselves off the market because they were frustrated all together and became discouraged by women in their age group having unrealistic expectations. I get it! There are women who are in their forties and fifties who still believe they have the advantage in the sexual Marketplace and it can be a deplorable place for men to date. However, just as a 20-year-old girl and a 20-year-old guy is a mismatch made in hell, so are high-status older men who are dating women well in their 40's. It's not a match because in most cases, the man has the advantage and the women have very little to offer him long-term.

What I would say regarding men who are frustrated with women who are past their prime and still have high standards is: understand and accept that you are more than likely in a way better position than them and time is the great equalizer here. Those women will continue to age out, decline in income, and be single, while you have the potential to ascend to greater heights, status and wealth. Their age group is the most vulnerable and has the highest rates of poverty compared to single males and married couples. Attempting to date in this age group is usually a car wreck and your time would be better spent striking out with women in their prime. I would rather spend time striking out with women in their prime than striking out with women who have nothing long-term to offer.

Stop with the social conditioning that suggests that men should be dating women their own age. The only people who believe that idea are men who can't date women in their prime and women who are past their prime. If you think about it, those same older women who are guilting men for dating younger women most likely dated older men at some point in their prime.

OLDER WOMEN ON THE PROWL

Women have the ability to mate with a wide variety of men and feminism along with sexual liberation has opened the door to the possibility of older women sleeping with younger men. In fact, when women do this, they are celebrated in the public arenas while men are still considered perverts for doing the same.

Dating apps have made it easier for these sexual arrangements to take place. For men who are in their purgatory years and are struggling to bag younger girls, an older woman can make all of that sexual frustration go away with some of the best, unrestrained monkey double backflips that he's ever experienced. Sure, she may not be tight and just right, but what man in his mid 20's actually cares behind closed doors? What these younger men have to be cautious of is that this amazing sexual experience won't last if he happens to be persuaded into a longer commitment. I've had many coaching calls with men who have taken the plunge with older women, only to find out that she was an alpha widow or she falsely represented her sexual nature and has walled up once the relationship became serious.

For older men, older women can create comfortable

scenarios as well and give their feet a break from chasing those high energy younger women. What older men have to take into consideration is that an attractive older woman has managed to be on the sexual marketplace for 20-30 years with an advantage and came up empty. That is a testimony for a lot of bad decisions and missed opportunities on her part. She could be single because she lost her husband, but more than likely, she's still single because of her refusal to let go of feminist ideology prior to hitting the wall, she divorced-raped her previous husband(s), she hit her peak financially and is now struggling or she's a cock carousel rider looking to retire her P-sleeve and needs a safe landing spot. A nice man, who may still be earning and socking away retirement dough would suit her well. For a woman in this age, how lucky can she be to find a co-dependent, hopeless romantic male that is exhausted and needs a break from chasing around younger, more attractive women? Jackpot

PART

IV

AWAKENING

CHAPTER
10

THE DATING MINEFIELD

I'm often found in counsel with married people who are frustrated with their spouse or that are tempted by the sexual expressway that is open and available today. From the inside of their marital domain looking out, it can look like a full day at your favorite amusement park with limited lines. It doesn't matter if you're male or female, just about whatever you want can be had if you're willing to play. For those that got married a decade ago, this was not the single person's landscape. Text messaging may have barely been a thing if you got married prior to 2005, so imagine the advances in technology that have been made that allow casual hooks up to be possible. Instead of having to exchange numbers and making a phone call, there are dating apps, Instagram and direct messages (DMs), Kik, Snapchat, WhatsApp, Seeking Arrangements, you name it. What's more, you have access to men and women worldwide, not just in your community. All of this in the palm of your little hand!

Knowing all of this can make a missionary marital wife or a DadBod husband less appealing. With the ease of getting a divorce, it may seem worth it to leave the lazy, lackluster marriage bed and head out to the wonderful world of single life. But, let me tell you something. It may look like fun, but over time, bathing in a cesspool will kill you.

Dating is a minefield, a wasteland for a host of personal, psychological, financial, family, spiritual, and sexual issues that aren't quite apparent when you get that "It's A Match" notification. Many times, you can't believe how lucky you are when you match with the hottie that lives three miles away from you that you've never seen in your life.

For men, there is a wide variety of women and most of them will be of a wide variety. There will be a healthy supply of 49ers, women who are "4's" but want to be treated like "9's" that much to your surprise, will make you seem like YOU can't measure up to them. For women, every sexual fantasy of your dream is one swipe and a Google mapping away from selling you that dream of being piped down forever by the best of the best. Until 10:30pm.

Today's single life can be defined as: you can get anything you want, but most of the time, you end up getting more of what you don't want.

ONLINE DATING PROVEN TO BE SCAM

The Federal Trade Commission recently sued the owners of online dating service Match.com and others for using fake love interest to trick men into paying for subscriptions. Before this investigation, I talked extensively about online dating being a waste of time and a lot of men didn't agree with me because they were knee-deep in mounds of 49ers bliss.

Of course, there are millions of people that are going to get laid via online dating apps. Even the woman that is claiming to be unlucky in love and only meeting creeps is getting banged out when the night falls. Most men don't have the same luck, maybe because their standards are too high and they don't want to date or bang any 49ers. If that's the case, then they won't have a lot of success and dating is a complete waste of time. If you want to bang out 49ers then online dating services are a rest haven for them. The problem is most of them inflate their value and want to be taken out on dates, they want to be catered to, they want to talk to you on the phone for hours and days before you meet, then waste your time or flake out on you. That time would have been better spent working on something that would benefit your life.

Now, back to the FTC lawsuit against the online dating services Match.com, OkCupid, Plenty of Fish and other dating sites. They are alleging that the companies used fake love, interest, and advertisements to trick hundreds of thousands of customers into purchasing paid subscriptions. Where's Serena and her financial abuse argument?

Men continue to be scammed, financially abused and tricked out of their resources in order to see if these love interests on these dating sites are genuine.

"We believe that match.com conned people into paying for subscriptions via messages that the company knew were from scammers. Online dating services obviously shouldn't be using romance scammers as a way to fatten their bottom line," said an official of the FTC.

Ashley Madison, which is the online affair hookup place had a leak in their system where every man who had signed up with them was exposed. It was also revealed that 99% of the women's profiles on their site were fake profiles. That's how crazy it is for men out there who are attempting to chase free P-sleeve. They end up paying in the end.

APEX PREDATORS - SCAMMING MEN

If you are not a strong red pill minded man, you will continue to fall for cases of women online using you for one of your resources: time, energy, money, attention, or status. Men are easy marks for women who are predatory or are simply wasting time to alleviate boredom in their lives. This is why red pill knowledge is essential for all men.

If you think you're the only man that is vulnerable to women wasting their time or targeting them, the NBA and the NFL are full of high-status men who fall for the same tricks. These men are all experiencing the same realities of modern relationships, feminist ideology, dating scams, affairs, out of wedlock pregnancies, divorce culture, manipulative women, child support and alimony laws, women using them for dates, and women dating multiple celebrity men. No matter how you slice it, all men deal with the same issues.

THE COST OF DATING FOR MEN

A lot of men are wasting endless amounts of money in the dating minefield; some of us are committing dollars that we don't even have rolling the dice on instant sex, romance and/or love.

Some of us are living paycheck-to-paycheck, desiring bigger and better things in our lives and at the same time trying to remain on the field. We're cold approaching women, scouring dating apps and even going on seeking arrangements to scratch that itch. We can't even get our money right, yet we're frustrated by the fact that women are trying to collect resources that we don't have and refusing to give us attention because we don't have it. The reality is that if we lose $50 a month on dating, that is $50 a month that we can't afford. You simply can't be out here broke dating.

But, let's take a close look at how much you can save in a month by staying off the field and focusing on yourself. I've outlined this point in my first book, Free Agent Lifestyle, but let's drive the point home here.

Men can easily spend up to $50+ a month on several dating apps' premium features to access a wide variety of women. However, after hours of swiping and messaging multiple matches, it essentially comes at a loss when you factor in the energy and focus that it takes away from the things that really matter. Now, let say you want to meet up with a few of the matches on your dating app. Most men hope that these women would want to jump right into bed, but that is not the case for 80% of men. From this point, you have to gas up the car, pay for Uber or public transportation and the reality is, unless you live in New York City, you better have a vehicle if you're out here trying to date. $40 in the tank sounds about right for a round trip from your house to the local eating spot.

Depending on how well you're trying to impress your date or if you're just dating low hanging fruit, you might not spend more than $15 on your look, but if you aim to impress and want to date outside of your league, you might be looking at $200-$500 by the time you add your outfit, a haircut, a shave, a wristwatch, your Louis Vuitton belt and a pair of Steve Madden shoes.

Now, are you going to meet her for coffee, lunch, or are you going to meet her for dinner? You're talking about from as low as $10 bucks all the way up to $150-$200 if you're going to be out there dating seriously. You are already at $500-$1000. Of course, you can use some of these items for multiple dates with different women.

You've finally completed the date and if you were able to get her to your place to do monkey double backflips all over you, then you got something out of it. But if you didn't and you drop her off at her home or at another mall where she can wait for her 9:30 pm date, now you just lost five hundred bucks.

In order to lift her spirits and lower her inhibitions, a cheap bottle of wine for $18 or an expensive $250 bottle might help your cause. Just have your consent forms ready. You can count your Netflix or Pandora subscription at $20, your special smelling candles for $15, and your $80 bottle of cologne. These things add up fast. Now we're at $800-$1250/month just to get you on the field, you're not even in a relationship yet!

In the meantime, I'm over here saving $1,000+ per month by staying off the field right now and you're struggling, pinching pennies trying to patch up your rent money for the month. Some men wonder how they can make a better life for themselves, but they're also spending a chunk of their money to entertain multiple strangers on dating apps.

Let's take into consideration the guys who say they are cutting corners and don't "pay for women." I'm going to assume that they're dating low hanging fruit or they are Chads or Tyrones, the exceptions to the rule for the majority of men. But, even those men get tired of banging 49ers and want to date up and they simply have to be willing to spend money to do so.

My projected total to date just a couple of women

during the month would be $800 to $1,500 per month and that's just for a few nights out. If you plan on seeing any or all of these women for a second or third time, this is going to require a lot more of an investment. You can't wear the same shoes and clothes, eat the same food, consume the same wine or wear the same haircut again. Most of these are recurring costs and most women aren't just going to start banging your brains out for free and shut off other opportunities to get fed and entertained. This stuff adds up and many guys are underestimating the amount of money that we spend just staying out there and it will continue to eat at your budget and your energy. With the right focus, you have the opportunity to turn a $500 investment into a $100,000 opportunity. Sure, there are times when you can get dates on the cheap side but not often and certainly not with higher status women. Most of the time you have to make an investment and I am telling you guys if you're not where you want to be in life, it's probably better to take yourself off the field at least for 3 or 6 months to see how much money you can actually save. Then you'll see that you can turn that money into more opportunities for yourself.

It's easy to get frustrated with entitled women that insist that you pay to play, but that should be expected to a certain extent. We already know what the game is.

Dating is kind of like leaving the air conditioning on with all your windows open, sure it still feels good at times, but at some point, you have to realize that you're leaking money.

I DON'T DATE. HERE'S WHY?

I do not date and I do not have any interest in dating at

this point in my life. As you can obviously deduce from this material so far, dating is not a high priority in my life. I've offered you guys some advice about what it cost to date and add that to the double standards regarding women wanting to be "progressive" in their lifestyle and hold onto feminist ideology when it suits them, and then do a complete 180 degree turn and talk about how men should still pay for stuff, that is unacceptable to me.

One of the benefits of sexual liberation and the removal of shame for women who live debaucherously is that it is easy to get P-sleeve without having to date. When you're used to being able to get it easily you don't have any incentive to pay to play. This is one of the negative side effects of sexual liberation. The argument of why men are considered studs for sleeping around and why women haven't always been is because women simply do not provide much value today and the one thing they have that is of value is given away frivolously on the cock carousel. All of a sudden, men don't have an incentive to date because the need to pay for high mileage P-sleeve simply isn't there.

Dating has always seemed to be something that you would do with someone you were trying to become exclusive with, not someone you're just getting to know. Also, with the availability of multiple suitors, women are not in the mood to be exclusive with anyone. There is no reason for them to be exclusive when they can get gifts, cash and prizes, attention, time and money from multiple men. Unfortunately, many men have figured this out and have removed themselves from dating altogether. Women have used every trick in the book and called us every name at their disposal to get the so-called "good men" back on the marketplace. However, these good men know that if they're dealing with women between the ages of 35 and 50, they've "been there and done that." They've "had their fun and want somebody serious now." They want to settle down with the "good man" who will accept her multiple flops on the marketplace now that she is approaching the wall at warp speed and losing value. The "clean up" men have left the marketplace and that has left many cock carousel riders and student loan debt holders with plummeting SMVs in a lurch.

The reality is that dating is just not fun for many men. Of course, there are going to be outliers, men who enjoy the entire process, but again those are the exceptions to the rule. There will be times where there is a little bit of fun, some laughs and entertainment, but with the expectations placed on men for dating, they are basically the event organizer and entertainment provider for the evening. When you're the trip organizer, you're not focused on having much fun, you're more focused on organizing the event. You're planning when and where you need to be at certain places, whether you're going to the museum, meeting for mini-golf or rendezvousing at a restaurant. You're making sure she's going to be ready at a certain time or not going to be late or flake on you. You're making sure that that reservations and the meeting times are accurate or you've purchased a ticket to the movies or sports event in advance and planning parking, monitoring traffic, and finally, you're making sure you have enough funds to pay for it ALL.

These are the basic expectations for dating so-called high-quality women, however, this is not what I'm not suggesting men should do. This is why I don't date.

Once you're on the date, you have to manage it. You're creating the atmosphere, making sure that the ambiance is right, making sure you're saying the right things, that she's laughing and entertained, that you have the proper clothes and making sure she's wearing the proper clothes to the event or location. All of this organization is a major commitment and you are setting the bar to all future interactions. Most men aren't having that much fun, as they are trying to manage the date.

In the end, all men hope they are going to get something for all of that effort other than conversation and a pat on the back. If done well, the receiver will have had all the fun and it cost her a couple of hours of prep time, hair products, a few pounds of makeup, overpriced shoes, and handbags that we don't care about. If he slips up on one of his duties or requirements, the date yields nothing. To make matters worse, society has conditioned him to expect nothing in return for his effort. If there is no connection, he does this over again until it pays off. On the other hand, she does the same thing, gets what she wants and then when she's bored, she shows up empty-handed ready to be entertained. That is quite the investment for a person that you don't know. I don't even give my friends this kind of quality time.

The lack of exclusivity is a major issue for most men. The fact that she can make this exact same arrangement for 30 days in any given month and turns men into nothing short of Foodie Calls. Before social media and dating apps, the average woman could have three or four guys that she might be trying to figure out, filter and be exclusive with. In order to be one of those, you have to see her at the mall, approach her, shoot your shot and demonstrate enough game to get her phone number. Then you have to leave a message or two on her answering machine, listening to her speaking soft and seductively to Jodeci music playing in the background. Then you have to wait for her to call you back. She might have enough time to be dealing with three guys at the most with that turnover rate.

However, today most women, including the 49ers have access to 300-3000 guys! You're dealing with everybody on her Instagram, everybody on Tinder, everybody on Bumble, everybody that is willing to approach her, everybody at her job and every man that is willing to give attention to even the slightest attractive women. The odds are stacked against you and even when you shoot your shot and hit, you get the opportunity to take her out, you're still battling hundreds of guys, hundreds of beta male orbiters and hundreds of fans. There's no exclusivity and if she's bored, she may just be taking you along for the ride.

Back in the day, you can pay $50 for a date at TGI Fridays and you might have a chance to see her the following week. But today? You're expected to pay $100-200 just to meet her and by the time you end the date, she's on Instagram commenting on bodybuilder's photos and responding to 200 DM's and worse yet, getting dropped off at her booty call's house with a full belly and a "fun" night out.

The reality is you're pretty much wasting your time and the guy that she is doing Monkey double backflips on is not taking her out on dates. The deck is stacked against men, and women have the advantage initially. Why would you continue to do these frivolous activities; pay money and waste time to do something with a woman that won't guarantee any amount of exclusivity.

Don't listen to these women that are 35-45 years old suggesting that what I'm telling you is wrong, crying "this is what's wrong with men today." They've already been on the cock Carousel for the past 20 years, have multiple men in their body count, and they want to dictate to us about what men need to do. They should have cashed in on their value on the marketplace a long time ago.

FEAR OF MISSING OUT

When you choose to stay out of the dating minefield, you will constantly be encouraged through fear and intimidation to return to the plantation. There will be name-calling, people will call you a quitter, people will instill fear into you, suggesting that you might miss out on a good opportunity. This is called FOMO or Fear Of Missing Out. The lottery system, some religions, dating coaches, colleges, dating websites and those that benefit from men being on the field capitalize on this tactic.

Sometimes, our curiosity or insecurities work against us and we believe that since we're not playing the game we may miss out on our sole mate or meeting that nymphomaniac at a bar that's going to screw us as we've never been screwed before. And, I'm not talking about screwing over our lives.

They're painting a rosy picture of good relationships and the great times that everyone experiences at the beginning of relationships, but they're not telling the entire story. All relationships end. Those that don't end, turn into marriages where 60% of them will end. Once you've done that a few times in life, other lifestyles become the priority. It is not to say that bitterness or hurt will lead to making this type of a decision, rather it is more of a cost/benefit analysis that does. As many have said, the juice isn't worth the squeeze and logical thinkers are willing to sacrifice the small bit of joy that comes with risking a whole bunch of pain. Feminism has made relationships even more difficult so some men have moved on to enjoying things that can guarantee them joy.

When I go to certain restaurants, I typically order the same thing off the menu because I am certain that I will enjoy it. My friends will say "You should try this dish or that dish." However, the risk of wasting my dining experience on something that I might enjoy isn't worth it. I'll stick to the menu item that I know will bring me joy.

The truth is, those who want you to have FOMO are usually projecting their fears upon you. Do not let the fear of missing out walk you into traps that your logic is telling you to avoid.

CHAPTER
11

THOT NATION

There used to be a time where you could tell the difference between a hoe and a housewife. Today, the lines are blurred as to who is a respectable lady and who is a street hooker. In most places in America, they appear one and the same, and sometimes the virtuous women are the most exposed. Women have taken their freedom of expression and ability to represent themselves without the expectation of judgment to the absolute limit. They can dress like strippers in public or online, collect the accolades of hundreds of thousands of strangers on social media, then turn around and claim to be a victim of misunderstanding when people treat her how she looks. The irony is that while women are walking around in their most exposed state ever, we are hearing the most complaints about men being creeps, sexual harassment, sexual assaults and rapes than ever before.

PLAUSIBLE DENIABILITY

We all have a story about a woman who is wearing a low cut top with her cleavage presented perfectly below the average man's eye level. Whether you are a man or a woman, we've all have been caught taking a sneak peek at a nice jiggly pair of exposes breasts. I mean, aren't they set up there for that purpose?

Well, apparently not! Because each one of us also has a story about this same woman with the exposed breast, complaining about catching you looking. "Hey, mister! My eyes are up here!" This awkward moment led most of us to immediately dart our eyes back into her scowling face with not much to say because we were indeed guilty. But after a few moments of clarity, our thought immediately goes to what we should've said at that very moment. "Of course I am, you've got them sticking out for everyone to see! WTF?!"

For the few men that were able to deliver that message with perfect time, good for you. Because shortly after, you probably got a lecture about being creepy for checking out all of that exposed skin and how she has no other choice but to wear tops like those and how she's not doing it for attention. We know better though; she clearly is using her breast to yield free attention and validation, which is the currency that women care about the most. It's a cheap trick and we hear a bunch of them when it comes to women and "wearing the hooker's uniform" as comedian Dave Chappelle would say.

All of the shaming language and deflection that women have come up with to pass the accountability back to men when overexposing their assets backfires on them. From "No Slut-Shaming" to "Women aren't asking for it" to "Just because I dress like this..." to "Teach your sons not to rape," have all passed the buck back into men's lap for an action that women decided to take on her own. They chose to wear the most revealing clothes in order to rack up attention points and then complain about it when the attention comes in from ALL corners.

This plausible deniability has opened the flood gates to more and more blurred lines between an honest, clean and wholesome girl and a straight-up attention thot. From low rise jeans to thong thong thong thong thongs. From booty shorts to push up bras, from tank tops to tube tops. From tip shirts to yoga pants, feminism has allowed women to find just about every way to expose themselves in public and not be called out on their indecency. It's one thing to see this in the shopping malls of America, but this type of attire ends up creeping its way into professional settings, as women push the attention whoring to any level possible to gain an advantage.

The people who actually get penalized are the men who get caught looking. Men at work, male teachers and administrators at schools, male students in college classes, men in grocery stores and male gym-goers all may find themselves having to explain their behavior when a scantily clad woman parades her assets into every male space imaginable. It's to the point that many women don't have professional attire, showing up to job interviews as if she just left a nightclub. Also, the men who complain are immediately shamed for pointing out an obvious flaw in our so-called "equality" society. Because all of a sudden he's "gay" for identifying what would be a crime if he pulled the same act.

This attention trotting is intentional. We've all heard about the woman who cries and exposes her cleavage to police officers after being pulled over in order to get out of receiving a ticket.

Even still, women use plausible deniability to naive men to explain away her drive to distract men or garner attention. At a moment's notice, what can surely be described as being a whore can turn immediately to "men are making me uncomfortable" and "I'm just wearing comfortable clothes."

Hoes are winning!

AYESHA CURRY PROVED THAT THERE IS NO HOPE

Even the nice girls end up wanting to join the Thot Nation. In early 2019, Ayesha Curry proved that she could possess several of these feminist hoe tendencies: competitiveness, the desire to seek attention from men other than her spouse and the slightest hint of feminist hive mindset.

Ayesha Curry is the wife of Golden State Warriors basketball player, NBA champion and two-time league's most valuable player Steph Curry. He signed a very hefty and lucrative $201 million dollar contract a few years ago and received several endorsement deals that pushed his income into the stratosphere. As a result of his high profile character, he has been able to open the door for his wife to pursue a career on camera.

They could be the poster family for NBA couples. The wife has kept a very feminine and motherly appearance, even being critical of women who don't dress modestly via her Twitter page. She focuses on their children while Steph is on the road competing against the giants of basketball and even has a few side projects that feature her doing traditionally feminine things, such as baking and cooking. Steph is also a symbol of a good respectable husband, who doesn't get caught up in all of the nonsense and scandals that many pro athletes are susceptible too.

That year, during an appearance on an online talk show,

Ayesha revealed that although she loves her husband, she admitted that she wonders why she's not getting the type of male attention that all of the other women are getting. I'm assuming that she's talking about the local Instagram thot model type attention. I will say that she admitted that it was a weird feeling and expressed some shame for her reasoning, but the women on the talk show sided with her feelings and didn't set her straight. Sadly, for men who looked to her as a beacon of hope for women and promoted her to other women as an example of what could be in today's world, it was a rude awakening that confirmed for many men that women cannot be pleased and that there's no hope.

Not to mention the fact that she humiliated her husband on national television while he was in the middle of an NBA Championship series, which they would lose later in the week. This also proved what I talked about in the Marriage Wheel; every single marriage goes through the exact same situations, no matter how much you give her. At some point she's going to not be content with her life, everything that he's provided for her, she's not happy or not satisfied. So doesn't even try!

This is a prime example of what men fear the most about feminized, entitled American women. She has everything given to her by a hardworking man that appears to have been as honorable as he could to her. She has a beautiful family, beautiful daughters, what we believe to be a beautiful marriage, and as far as we know, a faithful NBA husband and the ability to do the things that she wants and enjoys. However, she's not happy because all the thirsty Chad's and Tyrone's aren't trying to lubricate her tonsils and offer her free monkey double backflips in their studio apartments. She's not happy that other men look at Steph Curry and his family with enough respect as to not interfere with their seemingly perfect arrangement.

The thot culture has not only affected many marriages of average people, but it has also worked its way up to traditional celebrity culture. If you have a loving faithful wife who you don't ever believe would cheat on you, Ayesha proved you wrong my friend. Worse still, she might have scared the piss out of every man who thought twice about marriage.

She has sent every man an open invitation to compliment her, give her free validation and offer her that male attention with any variety of low ball offer imaginable. It would be hard to take her seriously if she complained about it. This is the same situation that women put themselves in when they dress like hoes at the gym, exposing themselves for everyone to see, then complain about all the negative attention. This is psychological warfare and quite honestly, it's the result of treating the majority of women like adults, when they have exhibited childlike decision making. See, children don't understand or accept consequence, accountability, and responsibility; neither do women who engage in this type of behavior.

Her identity was as a traditional wife, a wife that we don't really see anymore in our culture and that's sad. While almost wife is trying to be a MILF, hanging on to the last of what remains of her sexual marketplace value or competition with her teenage daughter, Ayesha chose to dress traditionally modest. But apparently, it was all an act; she wants to join the rest of the Thot Nation and it seems that many women are looking to do the same.

She just got to the point of the bait-and-switch on the Marriage Wheel and no surprise, Steph had to come out and support his wife's comments simply because he had no other choice. If he didn't support her, it would have cost $100 million-plus, so he had to be the good boy and meet her at her level. She's having some feelings of insecurity because she understands she is near the end of her fertility window and the low point of her SMV, so she is instinctively virtue signaling to any potential mate that she could be available on the market should Steph succumb to any temptations on the road via his new fame.

This is why I tell you that marriage today has too many disadvantages and pitfalls for it to work today. People think that I'm making this stuff up sometimes. These things happen no matter how much money you have, no matter how much masculine frame you've got, no matter how much you lavish on her, they all have the same nature and that's just what they are. I'm not saying that they should be different, I'm just saying know who you are dealing with and don't write a blank check against their nature.

The reality is that Ayesha probably receives plenty of male attention. In fact, men have held her in very high esteem and placed her on a pedestal based on her image, but what she meant to say was "I'm not getting male attention from the type of men that I would like to get male attention from." That's what she should have said. She wants the studs, the Alphas, the Chads, and the Tyrones to give her the type of attention that they give these Instagram thots.

FULL EXPOSURE

A man today in his 30's has already seen more ass and tittles on a public street than all of the men combined in the three generations before him. Men used to have to crawl up in trees with a set of high powered binoculars and be the neighborhood peeping Tom to catch a woman in the slightest state of undress. And we're talking mere moments of skin being revealed. If he couldn't achieve it in public, he might've been able to get his hands on a Kmart ad in the Sunday newspaper to see women posing in cotton panties to get his rocks off. Today, he doesn't even have to leave his house. His smartphone has all of that and more. If he wants to see it in real life, he can just walk outside. Thots are winning!

ARE THERE ANY GOOD WOMEN LEFT?

When I say good women, I'm talking about feminine and sensual women, plain and simple. If I didn't know better, feminism was probably created to kill the constructs of sensuality and femininity simply because the typical, overweight feminist couldn't achieve it. The women who exhibited the highest levels of femininity were often selected first and taken off of the marketplace by higher status men. What remains are individuals who talk about equal partnerships, about what she brings to the table, which always ends up being a list of intangibles or things that cannot be measured such as respect, love, appreciation, vision, loyalty and of course, herself. When you ask women to do something feminine, womanly or nurturing, they will reject you and talk about not needing to do those things because she's strong and independent.

What's left are plenty of single mothers who have already freely given away what she's asking men to pay full price for. There are the reformed cock carousel riders, party girls, former strippers, coke whores and weed heads.

In years past, there was the saying, "You can't turn a ho into a housewife." This is sound marital advice that many men are missing out on today in dealing with modern women.

There are social media addicts and the women who are constantly advertising themselves for attention. The one who attaches her self-esteem to likes. You can't be in a serious relationship with someone like this.

The divorce culture has produced an unlimited amount of divorcees. 8 out of 10 divorced women were the ones that actually pulled the trigger on their marriage. Could she have good qualities? Yes, but if you get married to a woman that has been divorced, the likelihood of her divorcing you is almost 70% and on a third marriage it is close to an 80% certainty.

There are the competitive women who not only are going to compete with other men in the boardroom, they're going to be competing with you in the bedroom. Many times, these women are running around with more degrees than a thermometer, sitting on hundreds of thousands of dollars of student loan debt and have the nerve to believe that they can compete with men.

There's also the Beta Male Hunters, women who are intentionally looking for weak men to control and manipulate. You also have the debt passers, women who see marriage as a way to pass their debt off to unsuspecting men in the name of love. There are the overweight women, which in America could include over 70% of the available women. The average woman in the United States weighs 168 lbs! That's the average, so you certainly will have no problem finding women that are 250 or 300 lbs., acting like princesses on the dating market. Of course, you can expect that they'll be feminists. There are just too many women with bad qualities and unfortunately, feminism has its ugly hand up the ass of American women. Remember, some of these women can be one and the same, they can be all of these or one of these. And because men often have a scarcity mindset, they believe that the only women they can get are the ones they can change, but it never works out that way. So be careful out there, that's what you got left and it is better to be single than to be with one of these women. Trust me!

RAISING DAUGHTERS IN TODAY'S WORLD

The days of fathers marrying off their daughters are slowly grinding to a halt. A father can anticipate providing his daughters with some sort of financial benefit well into her mid 30's because feminism has taught them to do it on their own and many of them are faking normal, but struggling in reality. Many are receiving support from men or former men in their lives.

It's getting hard to provide your daughter with quality instructions to be a good, virtuous woman when these hoes are winning out here. It's hard to tell her that when her mom has succumbed to feminism, thot nation, and is operating under the spirit of Jezebel, while the father is at home picking up the slack with the kids. It's hard to tell your daughter to respect her body when every celebrity that she sees has sold her body via a sex tape or was a reformed stripper. Many of these young female celebrities will push the feminist agenda in their music with songs depicting that God is a woman.

You can do your best to try to educate your daughters,

but if they have a single mom, if they have a feminist behind them, if they attend a public school indoctrination camp or if they go to college, everything that you worked so hard for will be unwoven and erased at the snap of two fingers. You can equip her with the necessary tools to be successful in her own way, but they are constantly bombarded with a subliminal message from the media propaganda machine and it will be unraveled by emotional feminist ideology in 4-5 years tops. They will be preyed upon by feminists and kids that were raised with no fathers in the home, by women who flushed their SMV down the toilet by using their P-sleeve to get ahead and seek to have your daughters do the same. They're told that men are only out to oppress and enslave them, meanwhile, when they stop listening to their fathers, they end up being enslaved by others.

I wish you fathers luck in steering your daughters clear of an ideology that has more blood on its hands that all of the American war generals in the history of our country combined.

CHAPTER
12

THE DEBT DEMONS

STUDENT LOAN DEBT BROKE

Most single women are flat broke! Many women have been given the idea that they are free when far too many of them are in over their heads in student loan debt and consumer debt and are not even able to afford to live alone. I'm not talking about 20-year-old women. I'm talking about women in the early to mid 30's and older. Many of them are still living at home with their parents, and. oddly, judging the lack of economically attractive men on the marketplace.

For feminism, attending college was a feather in their cap. They perceived a college degree as a way for women to achieve equality in the workplace. Even when a feminist newspaper article celebrates the fact that the majority of college students are women, you have to scratch your head and wonder if they are ignorant of the fact that 67% of the student loan debt belongs to women. This has to be a major loss in the column for feminism. They were successful in producing the most debt slaves in a 50 year period.

Now, why is this important for men to accept and

understand? The answer is simple; young men are the targets for women to dump their debt into their laps via marriage. I've been emphasizing this to young men who are often blindsided by the realities of debt once they establish long term relationships and marriages. The reality is that a majority of women in the marketplace are flat broke and they are pretty much the predator when they are on the marketplace. They are looking for individuals to rescue them. They are not looking for love, they're not looking for lovers and sexual partners. What they ultimately want is an individual they can marry in order to get them out of the debt situation that feminism has created for them.

When women say they are looking for economically attractive men and are not finding them, their game was exposed. A lot of these women originally believed at the time when they were signing off for these student loan debts, they were going to find a simp to marry and have that simp pay off that debt. This was the original plan that was laid and many of these individuals who have laid this plan 15 years ago had a large marketplace of available SIMPs that were as ignorant as a gender studies professor in a debate. There were plenty of men who were flying blind and that had very little red pill knowledge. But, that has changed over the years.

Once men are in these marriages, they tend to commit to paying off these debts under the traditional beta male provider model. After the debt is paid, many times this can be the death sentence for their marriage. Many women have chosen to leave their marriage around the time a home gets paid off, when breast implants are paid for and when the student loan debt or consumer debt is zeroed out. This is when problems enter into the relationship and the exit strategy is ignited. If these debts aren't paid off, this is when she fights her ex-husband tooth and nail in the family court to try to find a way to get that debt passed on to him.

Unfortunately for them and the American taxpayers, the current relationship and marital market aren't the same as they were 15 years ago. Men aren't getting married at the same rate and this leaves a lot of women with debt hanging over their heads that they didn't intend to pay. Instead of buckling up and tightening their belt to help pay down this debt, they are looking to elect a presidential candidate that promises women that they will write off their student loan debt.

This is a very dangerous choice to make and feminists are now putting everyone's safety at risk once again for their selfish gain. This would be similar to a college football quarterback who owed his campus bookie millions of dollars. He is compromising the school, the team, the coach, and the alumni's authority and could be willing to throw games in order to settle his debt. These desperate debt slaves are willing to vote in people to major government seats that preach high levels of socialist ideologies. That is very dangerous to our freedoms, but a feminist never cares about everyone else, just about herself.

TEACHERS ON SEEKING ARRANGEMENTS

An article that was featured on Yahoo Lifestyle reported that female elementary and secondary school teachers are turning to Seek Arrangement and sugar-daddy websites in order to supplement their incomes. I guess gone are the days where a teacher would take a summer job during their two-and-a-half-month break. Nope, those jobs must not be available anymore. So, why not turn to the oldest profession in the world to make ends meets?

Of course, this article had a lot of boohooing and women playing the victim, having to moonlight on their backs because of the economy and declining teacher's salaries, along with the dubious gender wage gap. More women are complaining about a lack of money and making excuses for deciding to moonlight in the beds of older men.

Here's the deal, I'm not against women going to college, nor am I against women going to work. However, I am against women playing both sides of the fence when it's convenient. They continue to brag about going to college at higher rates than men, but end up choosing majors and jobs that won't make enough money to support themselves. Now it's everyone else's fault that she has to get pounded sex ways to Sunday after creating her weekly lesson plans.

One woman pursued a Ph.D. and was surprised that she was getting a low salary offer for her job. Now, because you don't make enough money in this profession that you CHOSE to go into, chose to invest your money in and you chose to spend considerable amounts of your younger, better and most fertile years doing, now you want to go do monkey double backflips on men of advanced age for money and then claim to be the victim. This is just retardation on steroids!

I actually don't mind if you decide to sell your P-sleeve on the open market. More power to you! But, once you put a price tag on that and a low price tag might I add, you cannot seek out an economically attractive, good man that is going to take you seriously in a relationship. Not when you've had a lot of guys running through you for money. You're not marriage material at this point, you're done!

What about the male teachers who aren't making money?! Are they able to make money the same way? Where's the equality on this issue? If female teachers are able to fuck for money on the side and male teachers aren't, wouldn't that constitute a gender pay gap? Would male teachers who were caught using the services of these female teachers on the website get the same sympathy and leeway?

It's clear that women simply do not want to get married anymore and so they can avoid being under the thumb or rule of a man in the house. They would rather deal with the government directly and what the government provides and as a secondary option, they lean back on their parents.

Women haven't been able to handle this so-called "Independence" and "I Don't Need No Man" movement very well because they've had nothing but dependency on the government. As a result, they've shown that they will be willing to give up every red-blooded American's freedom in order to bail themselves out of their bad decisions.

CHAPTER

13

THE RETURN OF MASCULINITY

Beta male behavior appeared to be the winning formula for almost three decades. They appeared to be rewarded well for it. They got the wife, the house, the kids and the in-home P-sleeve that they could occasionally tap into with a little effort and planning. However, if we look at how these men got treated, dragged to divorce court, discarded, abused financially, and became victims of paternity fraud, child support suits, payments for the past use of a marital P-sleeve, you have to ask yourself "Were they actually winning or losing the entire time?" Or "Were they winning AND losing at the same time?"

Think of the men who adopted the emotional characteristics of their single mother or followed the social conditioning of "the good guy." Those that sought to put the best interest of the woman higher than their own rarely had great stories to tell. After all is said and done, what many of them were the beneficiary of was getting stuck in loveless marriages, muted and silenced into compliance, subservient relationships, false domestic violence charges and alienation from their children.

A woman once said to me, in defense of her position, "Married men live longer than single men on average." It seemed like a valid statistic, but it didn't prove anything other than a woman providing yet another fear-based tactic to get men to comply and agree to be beta male providers for feminists. The statistic that proved her point said that married men can gain an extra 1.7 years, however, married women can knock off 1.4 years from her life. What is not known is, what does that extra year or two actually look like? Is he staying alive under obligation? Is this extra time peaceful or is he listening to nagging the entire time? Did he accomplish anything during that time? Did he live a fuller life compared to the man who remained single? Extra time lived under duress doesn't equal success.

MEN APOLOGIZING FOR BEING MEN

Everyone with eyes can recognize that feminism has had more negative impacts than successes. I don't care what wave of feminism you want to talk about, the lack of agency and responsibility has made supporting their causes unbearable. The prolonged psychological and emotional warfare that feminism has created has led to the idea that men should be less of what they naturally are and at the same time look at women as having the same qualities as a successful man. Qualities like bravery, fearlessness, and independence are all things that are achieved through masculinity, specifically sacrifice, risk, ingenuity, and strength. Nothing that feminism has accomplished has required any of these things. All that was required were for a group of men to be compliant and change legislation that would benefit one side and handcuff the other.

Equality, true equality is a myth and cannot be achieved. Even feminists know this because most of their agenda is to push for only equality in outcomes in certain career fields. We simply have to look at ANY statistical data related to strength, IQ level, college-based standardized test performances, agility, reaction time or ability to drive and it wouldn't take long to conclude that men are better at the vast majority of these skill-based or intellectual objectives. Those who are thinking with their logical brain already acknowledge this, however those who are on the emotional soul train would like people to feel different and not take the data into consideration. The equality push is basically trying to get you to believe that women can do these same things equally.

To prove their point, a feminist will do one of two things. They either highlight the few areas where they have the advantage and brow-beat men into accepting their inferiority in that area. Or, they will find the exception to the rule, a woman who is stronger, bigger, faster and/or smarter and put them on display to disprove the rule. Listen, more power to them and there's no way I'm trying to say that women are not good human beings, however when we talk about ability is multiple areas, the equality argument just falls flat on its face.

Men have slowed down their progress, ambition, success and drive in order for women to catch up. We see more and more men who are willing to be less masculine or older men apologizing for things that they've said in the past in order to make women feel better about themselves. This war has been unleashed on young boys, who despite having a clear and distinct advantage over their female counterpart, have to deal with the confusing equality discussion led by school where 89% of the teachers and administrators are female and they are disadvantaged by having the classroom educational procedures being suited to a female-style learning environment. All while the boys are more likely to be drugged by ADHD medication, pushed into special education and the programs that they enjoyed (physical education, music, auto tech, woodshop, etc.) are being stripped from the campuses. Courses like home economics that taught homemaking skills that would be beneficial to boys and girls were removed and the agenda to push girls into underrepresented classes like science and math was instituted. Later, college and university would lower the entrance requirements for women in order to admit them into medical, engineering and science programs.

We are seeing celebrities having to apologize for things that they said in the past or for exhibiting masculine behaviors that were fair game. This is equivalent to bowing down to the feminist and alphabet soup groups who have assumed power in media and entertainment in order to control the narrative.

These professional lobbyists and organized groups are controlling the mindset of women across the world and have made their dependency on them look like independence. They are able to make men look less masculine and prop up women like superheroes, whether it's the super mom, the super single mom, the super independent cock carousel rider or the super working mom who comes home and has to be supermom because the beta husband was "out to lunch."

The few men who had the guts to challenge this authority and talk specifically about the dangers of feminism, the #metoo movement and the dangers of raising young boys without having masculine figures, have been deterred from speaking. They have either been shamed into silence, knocked off of their platforms or got a little pressure from the feelings monsters and turned 180 degrees to apologize for telling the truth.

The old saying "If you give someone an inch, they will take a mile" sums up this movement. These groups have the free right to put dresses and fingernail polish on any young boy who plays with his sister's plastic doll on a Tuesday and proceeds to socially castrate him before trying to put any real masculine figure in his life as a remedy.

As usual, these "awareness" issues seem to arise when we are safe and protected. There is less of a need for masculine men because all is well. There are no threats that require women to put up or shut up. There are no physical wars and battles to win. There are no barbarians at the gate. As such, men are disposable and masculinity is not needed. Masculinity only gets in the way and prevents them from accomplishing what they want, all in the comfort and safety provided by masculinity.

We see this issue in the black community where it has essentially functioned as a matriarchy since the Civil Rights Acts in 1965. Women have chosen to rely on the government for support and discarded the men who either could not or would not support them. These communities are thought to be completely out of control, yet have the most women believing they are strong and independent. Women in these communities have no problems raising their children without the presence of men.

The young boys who seek to display masculine characteristics more often mimic the behavior of their single mother/mom wives. Ultimately, when there is danger in the community with gangs and drugs, when there is police brutality and when politicians start peeling back all of the handouts that they've been used to receiving, it is often the women who revert back to traditional roles and start calling for the men to protect and advocate. However, the men have already been emasculated and run out of the community or disenfranchised by government programs that women aligned themselves with.

Men are scared of women and are scared to display masculine traits around them. They are scared to voice opinions that are logically based. Over time, these women have been shielded from so much truth that men who talk like me are shocking.

There is a need for men to return back to masculinity because these times of comfort won't last forever. All it will take is a major economic event, a natural disaster, a World War, or simply for the light to go out for an extended period of time to see who takes the back seat first. Most, if not all of the "future is female" type of people will take their natural position and defer to men and will be seen running for safety chanting "women and children, first." All of the men who wore fingernail polish and dresses as young boys will assume the same position that women will when the Barbarians come to the gate and wipes this place clean. The women will do what all women have done in the past, lie on their backs and spread their legs for the alpha who actually takes charge and establishes true masculinity and order.

IS THERE A CHANCE FOR HEALTHY RELATIONSHIPS?

I was once asked by a woman who got a hold of my content and asked me if I believed in healthy relationships. To her credit, she's known me for quite some time and understood where I was coming from and didn't immediately shun me for my beliefs. She has always been very supportive of my ability to speak about these subjects.

Anyway, if we talked about psychologists who seem to control the narrative regarding healthy relationships, they are generally speaking about the benefits of living blue-pilled, traditional lifestyles that children can model in their future relationships. However, in our divorce culture, there's not a lot of healthy relationships to model. There are lots of dysfunctional relationships and far too many single mother run households where the young girls and boys don't get to see healthy relationships modeled. The norm today is relationships that are out of balance where both people are out in the field competing with each other, trying to survive in difficult economic conditions and then coming home and competing with each other. Nobody wants to come home to that and this leads to unhealthy relationships.

When the state decided to get their greedy hands into everybody's relationship and take ownership of the byproduct of those relationships, this also caused relationships to get out of whack.

Not only that, but feminism has injected into women's heads that men prefer career-oriented, strong, and independent women and that they will be much happier with these women and vice versa. When you add those three factors into relationships where the modern society believes that the dollar supersedes everything that we do, you have no possible way for the common person to have a healthy relationship. Of course, there will be outliers that make this situation work, but they are the exceptions to the rule and the divorce statistics back this up.

So, this is what I would say to individuals who might have gotten this far into the book and still concluded that maybe he's just jaded or he's just bitter. If you look at the statistical data, it backs up the fact that the majority of people are having problems trying to balance these alternating currents. We're trying to balance competitiveness in relationships, feminist ideology, and the fact that the state is banking on the possibility that your family will be destroyed by these factors. Most of the time, the state is hitting the pay window.

If you want to go deeper into this rabbit hole, we also have people who believe that there is a grander conspiracy, looking to eliminate normal traditional relationships. If you look at the media, they actually denigrate traditional relationships, family values, and stay-at-home mothers, while pumping up non-traditional relationships, dominant women and independent feminists. If you want to go even further, you can look at the depopulation agenda driven by the banks and the 1%ers, who have created groups of people who believe that there is no need for the traditional homes. What better way to accomplish this than by having men and women at each other's neck.

In modern relationships, there's no yin and yang. There's very little that one brings to the table that could benefit the other. You have women that are saying "I am the table" and at the same time saying "I will not submit." And men on the other side saying "well I don't need your table, I already have a table in my house."

There is a small segment of women who are looking for healthy relationships. Unfortunately, these are women that are past their prime and have already reached their peak income and are staring down the next 40 years of supporting themselves. What they are offering to men and the good guys who were looked over in the past, is a person who has been ridden six ways to Sunday by corporations and alpha men alike. These women are benefitting far more than the guy who is considering taking them in. Many men at this age are giving women the side-eye and thinking "oh, now you want to be compliant, now you want to obey, now you want a healthy relationship when you at the disadvantage on the sexual marketplace. These are not your best years and it's won't be the years that I would be willing to write a check against."

I am a very cynical but realistic person. I'm not a hopeful individual; I'm a very logical person. However, I'm hopeful that in the future, we can work around these situations in order to correct them. We've done so much damage to our future selves and never thought about the children who are going to model their future relationships based on the behaviors of the selfish individuals we have today. This is a recipe for the disaster in our future and we can blame nobody but ourselves. From my perspective, we can look at feminism, the greedy government, and those who are looking to benefit from non-traditional relationships. I'm not going to take the blame for refusing to participate in a lop-sided and fractured system. Looking into the future, "healthy traditional relationships" may be a thing of the past for our children. We're going to have a lot of people who are living by themselves, adult women living with female roommates, girls living in Vans making YouTube videos and men living the best possible lives that they can afford. That's where we're headed.

THE FUTURE IS STILL MALE

Every now and then, when I'm out at the movies or traveling, I'll see one of those shirts that say 'The Future Is

Female' usually worn by a relatively small, underweight woman who's been taking a few boxing classes in her suburban gym. I even see clothing stores selling these types of shirts and refuse to take them down even in the face of heavy criticism. I get a chuckle from it, but this is a dangerous form of drip propaganda and empowerment; it makes no sense.

Imagine a man walking around the malls of America with a shirt that read "MALE EMPOWERMENT," or "THE FUTURE IS STILL MALE." He would receive all kinds of negative comments and backlash from women and worse yet, white knights.

I imagined it, so I created it! I'm wearing a shirt right now that reads "The Future Is STILL Male," and created the lifestyle to prove it. This is the first-course correction that will put feminism back to where it needs to be. If you thought this course correction was heavy, wait until the next few.

ABOUT THE RESEARCH

This subject has been a passion of mine for over a decade and several people can testify to the fact that I've been discussing these issues long before some of my trials and tribulations in my personal life. Actually, one of my undergraduate academic papers was on the subject of Title IX and gender equity in college athletics. I've archived a large collection of articles, academic studies, a library of book titles, graphs and newspaper articles that supports the topics covered in this book.

If you want to dive deeper into what you've just read, you will find an extensive list of references and other data organized by chapter at www.gregadamsone.com. You will find links to articles, fun facts and interesting videos that will further enlighten you on this subject matter. Thanks for reading further and enjoy!

ABOUT THE AUTHOR

Coach Greg Adams is a father of two children, a YouTube personality, podcaster, author of two books, life/divorce coach and motivational speaker. This is his 2nd book, a follow up to the Free Agent Lifestyle: Men's Guide To Peace, Quiet and Freedom which was published in 2019. He has worked in the fitness industry as an independent fitness trainer since 2013 and a college basketball coach for over 15 years. He is featured on the Coach Greg Adams YouTube Channel and can be heard on the Free Agent Lifestyle podcast. For more information, please visit www.gregadamsone.com or www.thefreeagentlifestyle.com